MADE TO WEAR
Creativity in Contemporary Jewellery

Janice West

with a Foreword by Barbara Cartlidge

MADE TO WEAR

Creativity in Contemporary Jewellery

Lund Humphries Publishers, London
in association with The Lethaby Press,
Central Saint Martins College of Art and Design

First published in 1998 by
Lund Humphries Publishers
Park House
1 Russell Gardens
London NW11 9NN
in association with
The Lethaby Press
Central Saint Martins College of Art and Design

on the occasion of the exhibition *Made to Wear: Creativity in Contemporary Jewellery* at the Lethaby Galleries, Central Saint Martins College of Art and Design
20 April – 22 May 1998

British Cataloguing in Publication Data
A catalogue record for this book is available from
the British Library.

Hardback ISBN 0 85331 727 5
Paperback ISBN 0 946282 47 1

Distributed in the USA by
Antique Collectors' Club
Market Street Industrial Park
Wappingers Falls
NY 12590
USA

Designed by Chrissie Charlton & Company
Made and printed in Great Britain by
BAS Printers Limited, Over Wallop, Stockbridge, Hampshire

Front cover:
Scilla Speet
Armband and earring, 1997
New silver alloy

Frontispiece:
Dinny Hall
Earring, *c.*1994
Silver

Contents

Foreword by **Barbara Cartlidge**

Having been asked to write a few words by way of an introduction to this book, I feel somewhat undeservedly honoured, as I have to confess immediately that my own career has been little helped by anything approaching the present-day standard of training offered by Central Saint Martins College of Art and Design in London.

I can truly claim to be an ex-alumna of what were once two separate colleges: St Martins School of Art in Charing Cross Road and Central School of Arts and Crafts in Southampton Row. I attended St Martins for two glorious terms, just before the Second World War, for life classes and fashion drawing. Much later, from 1957-60, I studied at the Central School as a mature student, where I learnt the basic rudiments of jewellery-making. The Central School had by then lost some of its more illustrious artist-teachers and students, and its workshops were staffed by elderly, trade-trained and -orientated teachers. They endeavoured to impart some of their skills with pathetically antiquated resources to a mere handful of 'older' students and the so-called day-release boys, who by law had to attend an institute of learning one day a week while serving their apprenticeship in the workshops of the Clerkenwell area. I think there were just four or five of us ladies, aged between thirty-six and sixty-five, of which at least three merely used the class for technical assistance to make conventional and expensive jewellery. A couple of male mature students enrolled so that they could pop into the work-shop on odd days and use the facilities to make quick little silver pieces for selling cheaply in markets at the weekend.

However, all these shortcomings did not bother me. I had enrolled purely on impulse, planning to find an outlet for my creative urges and hoping to make myself a few baubles I could otherwise ill afford. I was a wife and the mother of two children at school, with no plans for a career or wanting to achieve anything approaching professional standards. I did not bother with diplomas, sit for examinations or acquire qualifications. I simply complied with the only compulsory demand: to make three or four pieces. I made a very simple pair of cuff-links in brass and copper, a copy of a Saxon brooch and a domed brooch with a wired overlay, which I completed within a few weeks. From then on, I could make whatever I wanted, asking for technical help whenever I needed it.

I began to make myself wild and wonderful (at least I thought so) jewellery of a kind I had not seen in shops or magazines. It was great fun, and soon friends and acquaintances were asking me to make pieces for them. Towards the end of my time at Central, the lady who ran the newly opened Craftsman's Market at Heal's bought a whole collection of my work, and a year later gave me the opportunity of a solo show which earned me a spate of publicity. It helped me launch a very successful career as a designer and maker of unique pieces of jewellery for nearly twelve years and I exhibited my work in Britain and abroad.

Although I had no problem as such with outlets, I felt that contemporary jewellery was a little lost amongst pottery and textiles in the arts and crafts shops. It seemed the right time for an independent gallery to devote itself exclusively to contemporary jewellery. With my husband's encouragement and backing, I opened the Electrum Gallery, London in 1971 to exhibit and sell my work as well as pieces by artist-jewellers from all over the globe. It has given me a wonderful opportunity to experience the joys and troubles of the jewellery world.

Why and how did it happen? The more I got into it, the more the entire subject of jewellery *per se* and its making began to fascinate me. I found out that there is more to jewellery than being mere decoration or a status symbol. Since time began, its attraction for people has been far more important in terms of its symbolism: as the supreme token of love and friendship, of belonging, its power as a talisman, or as the means to express the wearer's personality. Its deeper ramifications: its archaic associations, the actual need for something small, personal, but lasting, that little bit of magic and even immortality which can survive for centuries, is for me the most exciting aspect of jewellery. Jewellery goes far beyond its material value or even its technical execution. To acquire the skill and ability to create an artefact that can be so important to people is a true privilege. Personally, I feel very passionate about it. Undoubtedly, the fact that I was a mature student helped my ability to concentrate, seek and absorb information in depth without special guidance. For younger students, it is absolutely vital that training in all the technical aspects of jewellery is accompanied by a wide range of seemingly unconnected subjects. All the fine arts, history, literature, theatre, film and all cultural activities including travel, study of nature, science and technology can be incredibly useful in helping a student to understand what jewellery is all about.

This book provides an unusually comprehensive view of the many aspects of jewellery – from design and production to one-off, unique pieces. It follows some fifty staff and ex-students, relating their points of view in their own words. The study clearly illustrates that much has been done and achieved. Yet, I still feel that, seen in conjunction with the general state of the 'industry', there still remain large gaps in the teaching programmes and methods of colleges. I know that funding always presents problems in providing ideal facilities, but the development of the mind is as important as the skill of the hand; the artistic content must be equal to the technical excellence. It would not be amiss to add a little dose of practical marketing and plain business procedures to the mixture to ensure the successful launching of a young person into the exciting but demanding career of jewellery in the next century. Contemporary jewellery, like all other cultural activities, reflects the standard and level of our society and, to do justice to our day and age, we must equip students with the widest possible know-ledge and facilities so that they may practise their chosen profession to the best of their ability.

I hope I will be forgiven if I take this opportunity to recommend to those in the commercial marketing areas of jewellery that they should read this book and, if possible, see the exhibition. It would be a big advantage for them if they were to take a more active interest in the training processes of young designers and makers, and if they were to acquire a more adventurous and forward-looking attitude in the running of their own businesses.

Introduction

J ewellery, like clothing, is ubiquitous. The person who says that they do not wear any jewellery is probably discounting a watch, a badge, a sentimental object they carry around with them. Most enjoy or even glory in wearing, owning or giving the portable decoration that is jewellery.

The status of jewellery is affected by this attitude. The importance of jewellery is easily overlooked and yet it is so widely consumed.

The aim of this book is to look at the making and consumption of jewellery. The text concentrates on the jewellers themselves and their products. One might even say that the theme is the process of jewellery rather than a litany of companies or a procession of jewellery styles during the last thirty years. There are many books that discuss jewellery as an object or series of objects and have little relationship to the passion of making, the passion for materials and the passion of wearing jewellery.

The jewellers chosen are some of the most innovative, skilled and the most admired jewellers working in Britain today but most of all they are passionate about jewellery. For those who have moved away from jewellery into other areas of art and design, this passion and a related interest in the body has stayed with them. Therefore I have chosen to include as wide a range of jewellers and silversmiths as possible.

This book is not intended as a history of jewellery in the last thirty years or of the jewellery course at Central Saint Martins College of Art and Design. Neither is it a recital of the career achievements of the alumni: through interviewing jewellers who were students or who taught on the jewellery course (or both) over the thirty years from 1966 we have been able to look at the various ways that the practice of jewellery has developed over this period.

The approach was two-fold: first to allow jewellers to speak for themselves and give their recollections of the course, their ideas about their work, the materials they use, the status of jewellery, the structure of the industry and the delicate relationship between consumer and jeweller. Most of these interviews were conducted by Ron Stevens, who taught on the course from its inception until 1996.

The second strand is my own meditation on jewellery during this period. As a Cultural Studies Tutor for Fashion, Textiles and Jewellery, I have often been struck by the anomalous position that jewellery holds. It is allied to fashion and yet its status is very different. Few jewellers are household names, the notion of the hallmark is synonymous with quality and yet few know what a hallmark means. Jewellery does not have the clear industrial structure of fashion, where the greatest care is taken in *haute couture* and the newest ideas come from couturiers and designers or from the street.

There are four general categories of jewellery. The most precious, often commissioned is referred to as fine jewellery; studio or contemporary jewellery has been the area of avant-garde developments and experimentation; high-street jewellery, which at best tends to consist of watered-down versions of fine jewellery and is conservative in its use of materials, usually silver or low-carat gold; the fourth category might be described as unwearable wearables and is perhaps more an idea about jewellery than jewellery as such. These works rarely exist outside galleries and museums.

What does a jeweller do? A jeweller makes jewellery – it seems so obvious, but the term encompasses a range of occupations, ideas, materials and processes. The finished product may be created for the unrelenting use of everyday wear or remain passive under the glass and regard of millions of museum vistors. The aim of the course at Central Saint Martins continues to be to educate 'designer-jewellers' who have a skill and ideas and who also have a vision of design so that they have, in David Pye's words: 'The power to materialise a concept, the power to give concrete material form to what was previously an invisible complex (within the artist) of thought and feeling.'[1]

The ability to design must contain a strong element of communication. The audience or potential consumers of jewellery must always be a part of the conscious or unconscious equipage of the jeweller's creative mind.

The emphasis in this book is not on the visual elements of design or style but the preoccupations that have exercised jewellers and changed jewellery in the years between 1966 and 1996. This begins with the climate in the 1950s and early 1960s which dictated the direction of jewellery for the next thirty years, and leads onto discussions on materials and technique, the relationship between art and jewellery and between fashion and jewellery.

Note: The Central School of Arts and Crafts changed its name to the Central School of Art and Design in 1966. It then merged with St Martins to become Saint Martins College of Art and Design in 1989.

1   David Pye, 'Design Proposes, Workmanship Disposes', in *Craft Classics since the 1940s*, Crafts Council, 1988, p.86

Into
the
Sixties

Contemporary Jewellery Exhibition
Central School of Arts and Crafts, 1951

CONTEMPORARY JEWELLE

At the end of the fifties everything was set for a renaissance in jewellery design. Society was changing and people were assuming new roles in it. As individuals, each of us was seeking a new identity and jewellery, the most personal and intimate of the arts, is about identity.[1]

In 1961, The Worshipful Company of Goldsmiths mounted the *International Exhibition of Modern Jewellery 1890–1961.* It was curated by the Company's Artistic Director, Graham Hughes, whose objectives were, first, to stimulate jewellery design by staging an exhibition which was truly international (exhibits came from Brazil, North America, Europe, India, Australia and the Far East) and second, to reflect all aspects of fine jewellery design and manufacture and to provide cross-fertilisation between artists and jewellers. To this end, such artists as Michael Ayrton and Elisabeth Frink were commissioned to produce jewellery for the exhibition using a wide range of materials. Teachers and students from the Central School of Arts and Crafts were also invited and Mary Kessell, Merlyn Evans and E.R. Nele created work which was later bought by the Company. Young jewellers who were subsequently to work at Central such as Gilian Packard and David Thomas were also asked to contribute. The policy of buying jewellery for the permanent collection at Goldsmiths Hall in London dates from this time and has proved a constant stimulus to jewellers ever since.

The show set the tone for the 1960s' new enthusiasm for jewellery of all kinds. The skill and imagination of the designer and maker became as important as the value of the materials. Ron Stevens remembers that Graham Hughes's achievement in this field was built on the earlier work of his father, George Hughes, who also curated exhibitions at Goldsmiths Hall. In the early 1950s George Hughes visited art colleges and talked to students to encourage a greater interest in, and knowledge of, jewellery and silversmithing. In 1963 Graham Hughes noted a major change in the public perception of jewellery, signalled by one event which represented a breakthrough in the appreciation of jewellery design and the status of the jeweller.

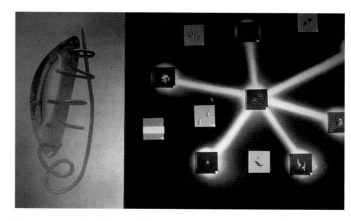

Contemporary Jewellery Exhibition
Central School of Arts and Crafts, 1951

On Tuesday 23 August 1963 Christie's made history. The world's oldest art auctioneers, founded in 1766, they were used to this, and the half empty room in King Street, St James's, certainly did not look unusual. But this was probably the first time that a truly modern jewel has ever been sold second-hand for more than the cost of its mineral content. A sixty-year-old masterpiece by Georges Fouquet, which, if melted might produce £30, actually fetched £420. The oft-repeated but cynical claim that the true value is melting value is at last proved wrong. The artist does matter: his impact on jewels is now apparent to the accountant as well as to the aesthete.[2]

This set a precedent for the selling of jewellery through the great auction houses and some might argue that the auction houses were the most conservative of bodies when it came to jewellery. Nevertheless this event was noted by Graham Hughes as the ultimate evidence of change. It meant that jewellery and the jeweller's art had a value that was dependent upon ideas and execution as well as upon material worth. It was truly a shift in the perceived meaning of jewellery, a shift from jewellery as portable display of wealth and status, or its role as handmaiden to fashion, into an independent area of design and art.

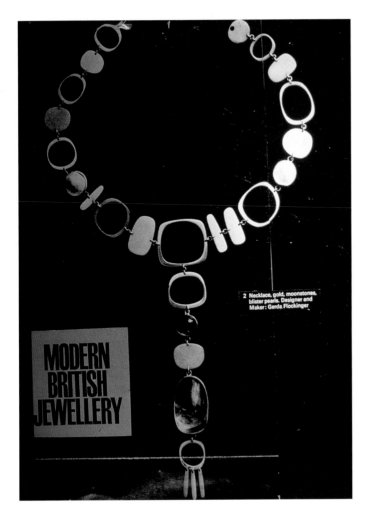

2 Necklace, gold, moonstones, blister pearls, Designer and Maker: Gerda Flöckinger

Gerda Flöckinger
Pendant, 1963
Featured on the cover of *Modern British Jewellery*,
exh. cat. The Worshipful Company of Goldsmiths, 1963

This change of emphasis had also developed in an educational direction when, in 1965, at Hornsey College of Art in North London, Gerda Flöckinger had set up the first jewellery course that transcended the idea of craftsmen training for the established trade. Instead the course was experimental and concentrated on the production of individuals who were able to create jewellery out of a personal response to materials and ideas.

Flöckinger studied as a painter at Saint Martins College of Art before considering jewellery. She studied etching, enamelling and jewellery design at Central between 1952 and 1956. Although she worked in precious metals, her handling of gold, silver and precious stones still has a distinctive freedom which transcends the traditional limitations of the materials and made her sympathetic to innovative uses of materials and ideas about jewellery and its wearing.

Reading the Jewellery and Silversmithing Department entry in the Central School of Arts and Crafts prospectus of 1963–4 it is easy to imagine that the course existed solely to train apprentices for the jewellery workshops in nearby Hatton Garden, which was the traditional jewellery and silversmithing quarter of London.

> The object of the school is to train students to enter industry. Instruction is given in traditional and con-temporary methods of production. The appreciation of fine design is developed. The school is in close contact with industry, which encourages students to study modern conditions and requirements.[3]

The school provided a one-year pre-apprenticeship course in silversmithing, jewellery and engraving, a three-year full-time course leading to a National Diploma in Design and a Central School Diploma as well as day-release courses for apprentices employed in industry.

However, the old course was more radical than this suggests. Just after the Second World War, the students had been taught by such tutors as Naum Slutzky who had worked in the Dessau Bauhaus. His radical use of materials such as chromium-plated brass and slabs of gemstone resulted in the creation of streamlined modernist jewellery never seen before. The artists Richard Hamilton and Patrick Heron worked there in the late 1950s and early 1960s. Barbara Cartlidge, Director of Electrum Gallery, writes:

> In Britain only a few art schools offered courses in metalwork or jewellery making ... the Central School of Art and Design in London was perhaps the most

important in those early days; its students were to make a name for themselves subsequently: among others, E.R. Nele, Gerda Flöckinger and later Susanna Heron. The Principal at the time, William Johnstone, asked artists like Mary Kessel and Alan Davie (both painters) to take an active interest in the Jewellery Department in order to stimulate amongst the students a more art-oriented attitude to their subject.[4]

However, these tutors had only a relatively small impact on the course and were resented by the Craft staff for their interference.[5] Individual students benefited from their contact with these artists but the course was taught with a close eye on the trade and it was considered more important that students should be able to make reproductions of antique jewellery and metalwork from technical drawing, usually provided by someone else, rather than designing it themselves.

The Government's Coldstream Report into Higher Education of 1961 had a massive impact on art and design education. The recommendations included a nationally recognised degree-level qualification and a new emphasis on design. Change was inevitable even where the old trade courses in jewellery and silver-smithing had become successful art-and-craft hybrids.

In 1965, the changes were announced in Central's prospectus:

> For many years the Central School has included Silver-smithing and Jewellery work in its curriculum. In the reorganisation of the School all classes previously in this department will be transferred with their staff to Sir John Cass College, Whitechapel Road, Aldgate E1 ...The Central School will start a small department concerned mostly with Jewellery Design for full-time students only, beginning in September 1965.[6]

The change indicated an ideological shift as well as a move from trade to studio jewellery. Design and the designer were in the ascendant and on 1 May 1966 the name of the Central School of Arts and Crafts was changed to Central School of Art and Design. The new course was not intended to be a copy of Flöckinger's course at Hornsey and was quite different in approach and content. The course at Central was created to develop the designer-jeweller. Inspired, in part, by Cellini's Renaissance goldsmith, the designer-jewellers created their own designs and also had the varied technical expertise to be able to make exactly what their imaginations dictated. Making and designing jewellery can hardly be called problem-solving activities in the sense that one cannot create, say, better earrings, only different ones. This led to an exploration of the wide possibilities of jewellery at Central as much as at Hornsey.

The removal of the trade course to Sir John Cass College created the space for a new kind of jewellery course. The new Principal, Michael Pattrick, approached David Thomas to lead the course. Thomas recalls:

> I was brought in to take over when Pattrick pushed out all the trade people. They were marvellous old crafts-men but very set in their ways. There was a need for good trade people, all the students that came out got jobs. But the art school was pretty disparaging of the jewellers. Pattrick came in and asked the staff 'How many of you have been to the sculpture exhibition at Battersea?' None of them had and he said: 'That's what I mean! You are just not interested in the arts, you don't understand all this and you've got to change.'

When Pattrick offered Thomas the job, he had just set up his studio in Chelsea and decided not to take up the post. Michael Pattrick then consulted Robert Goodden, Professor of Silversmithing at the Royal College of Art, who recommended Brian Wood for the post of Head of the School of Jewellery Design.

According to the 1966–7 prospectus, the new course aimed:

> ... to encourage an experimental approach to Jewellery design against a background of research into both modern and traditional techniques and forms. Critical

awareness, sensitivity to materials and an appreciation of the essentially personal character of good jewellery are fostered. Drawing from nature and the use of drawing in the design process are integral to the training.[7]

The relationship between the course and the industry was not to be lost however, with visits arranged to factories, workshops, museums, exhibitions and fashion houses.

To further his vision of the new jewellery course Wood appointed the following staff: Peter Lyon, sculptor and jeweller; David Thomas and Gilian Packard, designer-jewellers; Leo de Vroomen the craftsman-goldsmith and Ron Stevens, jeweller and silversmith who recalls:

Brian brought together the people who he thought really cared about jewellery and who could communicate this to the students. We came from a variety of backgrounds and all had our own ideas but Brian brought us together and created a dynamic and exciting course. We were all practising as well as teaching, for example, I was a partner in the Silver Workshop in Garrick Street for some years, so we really understood every aspect of the business as well as being immersed in art and design.

Neville Morgan, who had worked as a staff designer for the Rootes vehicle group and as a product designer for Robert Welch in the 1950s and 1960s, remembers being approached by Wood to work as a technician on the course. 'But after a year Brian said he would rather use me as a tutor. He wanted me because I had all-round industrial design background experience and I had a different point of view from the straightforward jewellery or silversmithing background. I brought a sense of design not channelled by idiom.'

Brian Melrose Wood was born on 27 May 1932 in Grassington near Skipton in Yorkshire. After attending Ulverston Grammar School he went to Lancaster and Morecambe College of Art where he studied illustration and silversmithing. He was fascinated by

Ron Stevens
The Everest Trophy, 1953–4
Silver and wood
Woodwork by Ron Stevens, metalwork by Naylor Bros

Ron Stevens
Pair of bowls, 1971
Silver set with pre-decimal British coins
Commissioned to mark the introduction of decimal currency for
Emmanuel College and Selwyn College, Cambridge

every kind of work in metal from jewellery to mechanics and hesitated before specialising in jewellery.

Brian Wood's training at the RCA provided him with the techniques and skills he needed as a jeweller and also with the contacts which later helped him to develop the course at Central. Professor Robert Goodden was impressed with his work and with the quality of his personality. He finished his time there by winning a silver medal for Work of Special Distinction and his work is held in the RCA collection. Wood was made a Freeman in 1979 and a Liveryman of The Worshipful Company of Goldsmiths in 1987.

After graduating he set up a workshop in Clerkenwell with his wife and worked as a freelance jewellery designer and maker. Most of his early work was jewellery made of gemstones set in silver. He sold his work through Liberty, Harrods, and the now defunct department store Marshall and Snellgrove. He also designed fashion jewellery for Mary Quant.

His wife, Margarita, was beginning her career as an art-therapist and invited him to teach at Goodmayes Hospital in Essex. Working with the mentally ill, he showed his aptitude for teaching by introducing the patients to basic techniques in metal and glass work.

When Wood joined Central in 1965, he found that Michael Pattrick was very much in tune with his own ideas on jewellery education. Pattrick thought that students should develop a comprehensive knowledge of materials and techniques and that they should have 'a sense of the structure and function of jewellery and what jewellery does on the body as well as understanding its social significance'.

Wood was also concerned that the students gained first-hand knowledge of other cultures and jewellery traditions. With the help of grants from the Worshipful Company of Goldsmiths, he was able to arrange field trips for students during the second year of their studies. The first trip in 1969 was to Bergen in Norway and to Pforzheim in Germany to study gem-cutting but also to see jewellery in a different context.

Margarita Wood describes her husband's approach to the students as: '... having a natural authority. He was in his way a benign patriarch and he was concerned with the welfare of the staff and students. He made an impact on the students in terms of benign containment, so that they felt secure and could concentrate on their work. D.W. Winnicott noted that a child could only learn to play alone, within a protected space. This was the start of creative life, so it followed that when students came to college, they should feel free to experiment in a secure environment. If they are pressured by all sorts of stuff – anxiety, lack of space and attention – then they cannot do their best and find it hard to attain true independence as artists and designers. Brian was up in arms when he felt that the quality of art and design education was being lost to accountants.'

Brian Wood remained an enthusiastic and dedicated leader of the course until his early death in 1991. One of Wood's legacies to jewellery education is the annual award of a travelling scholarship set up by Margarita Wood and now in the hands of The Worshipful Company of Goldsmiths. The first scholarship was awarded to Zoë Bunker who furthered her research into enamels at the Royal College of Art.

1   Peter Hinks, *Twentieth Century British Jewellery 1900–1980*, Faber and Faber, 1983, p.118

2   Graham Hughes, *Modern Jewellery: An International Survey 1890–1963*, Studio Vista, 1963, p.217

3   London County Council, Central School of Arts and Crafts Prospectus, 1963–4, p.22

4   Barbara Cartlidge, *Twentieth Century Jewelry*, Abrams, 1985, p.77

5   See William Johnstone's account of this period in *Points in Time, An Autobiography*, Barrie and Jenkins, 1980, especially the chapter entitled 'The Central School of Arts and Crafts'.

6   London County Council, Central School of Arts and Crafts Prospectus, 1965–6, p.20

7   London County Council, Central School of Art and Design Prospectus, 1966–7, p.48

Brian Wood
Alms dish, 1961
Silver
Made for St Paul's Church,
Grange-over-Sands, Lancashire

Brian Wood
Necklace, 1959
Silver and pearls
Maquette for Silver Prize piece at the RCA

Brian Wood
Wafer box, 1966
Engraved silver
Made for St Wilfrids, Barnwell, Yorkshire

Brian Wood
Ring, 1973
18-carat gold, diamonds and emeralds

Materials

Barbara Christie
Pendant, 1997
Gold and silver

The products of the goldsmith's art are intrinsically numinous. They have their place at the heart of every Mystery, in every holy of holies.[1]

The period between 1966 and 1996 saw a fundamental change in the nature of the production of jewellery. It was a period during which the traditional notion of jewellery being 'precious' was subverted. Fake or costume jewellery had existed for a long time but jewellery made from non-precious materials had traditionally consisted of copies, more or less skilful, of precious jewellery. Obviously there have been notable exceptions to this: René Lalique's use of glass and horn earlier in the century is a good example of a virtuoso's use of non-precious materials but his mastery might even be said to have dissuaded others from experimentation. Traditionally the essential worth of jewellery was that of the materials, not of the craftsmanship or design qualities of the piece.

Commentators such as the jewellery historian Peter Hinks ascribe this approach towards new materials to the result of high gold prices worldwide which made jewellery very expensive to manufacture. Although this was a consideration, in 1984 David Poston argued that the situation was rather more complicated.

> It has become a cliché that the use of non-precious metals arose from economic reasons. This was not true and has misled countless students and administrators ever since. Gold jewellery is where the money is since labour and design will always be a fraction of the cost of the piece, whereas in non-precious jewellery labour and design appear to be the only factors in the price. Non-precious hand-made jewellery therefore relies entirely on its design, execution and intellectual validity for success in the market place.[2]

The appreciation of the non-material worth of jewellery, its concept and design quality stems from a more design-literate audience as well as a shift in emphasis to design in jewellery education. It also coincides with the dissemination of one of the more useful ideas of post-modernism: that of pluralism.[3] The hierarchy of materials listed by Ruskin in the mid-nineteenth century reflected what had historically seemed a God-given order of materials and their qualities with gold as the purest both in property and in metaphor. The idea that so-called base materials might serve the purpose of gold equally well, or that materials traditionally un-related to jewellery-making might be used for body decoration and adornment, together with an ever expanding range of new materials, was a heady mix for any jeweller.

Peter Hinks gives different and more pragmatic reasons for the shift away from precious jewellery in the 1960s and 1970s when he points out that crime was increasing as individual wealth increased and many considered it reckless and tasteless to display wealth. The reduction in number and formality of Court occasions – debutantes, for example, were no longer presented at Court – meant that the rules for jewellery-wearing and, inevitably, jewellery-designing and making changed.

Poston's grasp of the economic reality of jewellery-making seems faultless, but as the experience of many jewellers and silversmiths in this book bears witness, it is not simply a matter of materials and skills. Poston's own reasons for eschewing the use of gold in his work were political. Most gold comes from mines in South Africa and is extracted in dangerous circumstances by exploited black labour. Often the size and exclusivity of a piece determines the financial reward to the jeweller. Many pairs of earrings will have to be made and sold to produce as great a return as one large piece of work. Making a large piece in metal is not simply a matter of making something larger; there is always a greater element of what David Pye calls 'the workmanship of risk' in a sizeable piece of silversmithing or jewellery.[4] As David Thomas says: 'If you are a potter or a glass-blower a piece takes you half an hour and if a piece does not work then you make another one. But it can take six months to make a piece of jewellery and if it doesn't work you've had it.'

David Thomas
Nautilus Cup, 1968
18-carat gold and nautilus shell
Commissioned by The Worshipful Company of Goldsmiths

David Thomas
Bracelet, c.1987
Gold and diamond bracelet with Chatham emerald and crystal

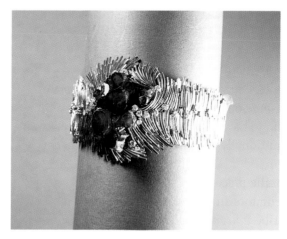

Georgina Follett
Necklace, c.1985
18-carat gold with rose quartz, enamel and ruby beads

Georgina Follett
Earrings, c.1987
18-carat gold and blue *pliqué-à-jour* enamel with opal hearts

Some ceramicists and glassmakers will feel that this fails to do justice to their craft, but if one considers work such as the silver and enamel vases made by Fred Rich then one can see Thomas's point.

Some makers choose to work in a material with which they seem to have an almost mystic bond. Georgina Follett chose to work as a jeweller because she was fascinated by work on a small scale and obsessed by working in three dimensions and in metal. For her, metal has a a sensual property that makes it seductive and compels her to make up the designs herself:

> I love the feeling of metal. Metal is to me one of the most beautiful objects there is. I love to touch some-thing cold that absorbs body heat. Two of the textures I hate most in the world are ceramics and wood. When I saw silver coming out of the acid and it was white it was love at first sight.

Follett's early work shows this appreciation of metal, scale and three-dimensional form together with a breathtaking use of *pliqué-à-jour* enamel. Nowadays, as Head of Design at Duncan of Jordanstone College in Dundee, she has little time for making jewellery but she transmits her passion for materials to her students.

Sara Pothecary stresses the importance of the com-missioning relationship in her work and that the jeweller is in a position of great trust:

> They like to trust a jeweller like their doctor or their dentist. People still believe that jewellery is worth the price because it's metal. Making jewellery is like being an interior designer, you are doing something special for someone.

There are others for whom the appeal of precious metals is not as visceral but is no less compelling. David Thomas worked for George Jensen for a year before returning to England to study at the RCA in 1958. He was dismayed by the emphasis on costume jewellery and spearheaded a return to the use of precious metals. He is an advocate of high-carat gold because of its superb handling qualities.

> I've always used gold. I think it's lovely stuff to work in. Gold is wonderful and precious stones are smashing. I like the scale of jewellery and these materials are super to work in. If you sit at a bench and use your hands and make things, gold always responds and no, you can't have a substitute and you can't work in nickel – you've got to work in the real thing. The whole thing changed in the 1970s when people went into plastics and paper and titanium, but it's very difficult to get the quality of real jewellery with those materials. It all went nutty with the Crafts Council trying to promote those kinds of people but they are trying to get back to more traditional jewellery now.

High-carat gold is becoming the material of choice for many jewellers. Dinny Hall and Wright and Teague only started working in gold in the mid-1990s and Margaret Turner, who owns two independent shops, is phasing out 9-carat gold unless she is asked to re-model it. The particular qualities of precious materials also appeal to John Volney: 'I want to get into more precious materials. I still like the idea of making really beautiful jewellery that is really different with a real design edge and that will become commercially successful too. I'd really like to reform public taste by producing work that is beautiful.'

For Ginnie de Vroomen working with gold has in itself been a source of inspiration:

> Gold has a special resonance for me; I am fascinated by the history and mythology involving it, and however much I know about the metal factually, its magic remains undiminished. The strength and malleability which gold possesses makes it the perfect material for our sculptural jewellery, formed by the *repoussé* tech-nique. Enamel has added another dimension to our work, enabling us to explore the joy of colour.
>
> My artistic approach combined with Leo's skill as a goldsmith, and the special empathy we share, has

enabled us to extend each other's talents. Through our company, *De Vroomen Design*, which employs many accomplished people, including ex-Central students Gisèle Moore, Oliver Fuller and Steve Lomas, we now enjoy the stimulus of marketing our jewellery internationally, whilst having the artistic freedom to create personal and unique pieces.

For Caroline Broadhead, the opposite is true. She started as a traditional jeweller but quickly found that metal was not her métier. However, she still suffered from doubt about the validity of her chosen materials.

> I remember making a plastic necklace thinking to myself 'God, this is silly, nobody wears a plastic necklace that's been crafted'. Plastic necklaces were just crap – they were just beads and children's necklaces.

Plastic is now seen as a legitimate and challenging material for jewellers but it has other drawbacks: it is dangerous to work with over a long period of time because of its carcinogenic elements and small jewellery workshops do not always have the highest standards of health and safety awareness. Other materials such as ivory and tortoiseshell have become unavailable to the jeweller as the species from which the materials are derived have been threatened.

Ron Stevens's response to a student's desire to use unconventional materials in jewellery-making was to demand that they prove or at least make a good case for their choice. One of his students, Reema Pachachi, remembers how passionate those discussions became:

> I remember having a dispute about whether or not wood was a precious material because I wanted to do something in wood. We might have disagreed on certain things but what was good and what was important were things that they cared about.

Clare Phillips has described the twentieth century as the century of the diamond and it certainly seems that in the last eighty years the diamond has been a byword for quality and worth in jewellery.[5] For many people, however, the glamour that surrounds the idea of the diamond is much more seductive than the stone itself. Diamonds were traditionally enigmatic stones, rendered as black spaces in sixteenth-century portraits because of the way they were cut at that time. They only sprang into life as the light hit them at certain angles. The use of diamonds for engagement rings is a twentieth-century phenomenon by which tiny shards of low-carat brilliant-cut diamonds are mounted to make the best of very little. In this way the unique qualities of the diamond are lost and replaced by a mundane grey twinkle which can easily be surpassed in brilliance by cubit zirconium. Some jewellers avoid using diamonds, possibly because the balance between pecuniary worth and the qualities of the stone seem at variance with one another.

Emma Paolozzi felt that diamonds were rather dull stones for a jeweller to use until she saw a bride at a particular wedding.

> The bride wore heirlooms, a diamond tiara and necklace. The wedding breakfast was in the evening and when I saw her wearing the diamonds in candlelight, there was magic happening all around her and it suddenly made so much sense. They were rose-cut, not brilliant-cut as modern diamonds tend to be.

Although the adamantine hardness of diamond has been traditionally associated metonymically with fidelity and strength, it can seem a cold stone. Paolozzi says that few of her private clients specify diamonds and they welcome her suggestions for different stones, cabochon cuts and unusual settings. She even persuaded one client to have a diamond set into the inner perimeter of a ring, a true hidden gem.

In Colette's story, *The Bracelet*, a woman has been given a diamond bracelet by her husband as an ostentatious and conventional anniversary present. She thinks: '"It's so pretty ... the diamonds are so white ... I'm so pleased ... Really, is a diamond actually as pretty as all that?" Then she let her hand fall back down and

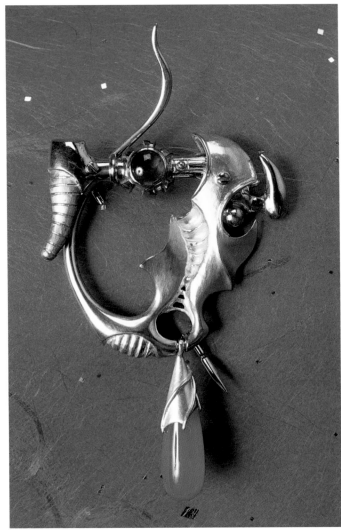

Margaret Turner
Fish brooches and bangle, 1996
Formed boar's tusk with tourmaline
From the *Deep Sea Collection*

John Volney
Jewel, 1996
18-carat gold and gemstones

Leo and **Ginnie de Vroomen**
Hair ornament or brooch, 1996
18-carat gold, enamel, diamonds and sapphire
Commissioned by The Worshipful Company of Goldsmiths

Leo and **Ginnie de Vroomen**
Bangle, 1986
Platinum, ebony and diamonds
Made for the Diamond International Award, 1986

Ginnie de Vroomen
Working as a designer trains one to see
differently: to analyse structure and balance
becomes second nature. Equally, experimenting
with form, colour and texture on a larger scale in
my painting enriches my approach to design.

Gerry Summers
Moonface, 1984
Gold, diamond and moonstone

Gerry Summers
After I left college I worked for David
Thomas and Leo de Vroomen; they are both
very good jewellers. I learnt rigorous
discipline and standards of perfection. My
work is precious: I only use 18-carat gold
and precious or semi-precious stones. Even
if I do more than one version of something,
they are always slightly different. I like my
work to be symmetrical, a symbiosis
between free natural forms and geometry.

admitted to herself that she was already tired of her bracelet. Madame Augelier craved a visual pleasure that would involve the sense of taste as well; the unexpected sight of a lemon, the unbearable squeaking of the knife cutting it in half, makes the mouth water with desire. "But I don't want a lemon. Yet this nameless pleasure which escapes me does exist. I know it does, I re-member it. Yes, the blue glass bracelet ..."[6] She has remembered the look and feel of the cheap but treasured possession from her childhood. This leads us to one of the most individual and important aspects of wearing and making jewellery, the meaning of the piece.

Simon Fraser is a jeweller who works in a variety of manners and with materials that are appropriate to whatever project he has in hand and he seeks to create jewellery which is directly concerned with emotion.

> For me, it is important that I make jewellery with meaning. I'm not really interested in exploring materials for the sake of it or working on ideas about jewellery. I'll work in whatever I think is appropriate to the project. I have no set method of working and I like to do something new and approach everything in a different way each time. I made a series of electro-formed rings when I was at the RCA. That's a great technique because every mark you make is reproduced perfectly, paradoxically the rings were about AIDS and danger and desire; not simply an exercise in metal and pearls. For Derek Jarman, I made a lovely long necklace of phallic flower bulbs which reflected his passion for gardening and which he buried in his garden at Dungeness. As for diamonds, I cannot understand why everyone doesn't use cubit zirconiums. What is the point of diamonds, I ask you? CZs are the same material, made in the same way, but not by nature and they can be treated in the same way by jewellers. It's only a rather dated version of 'romantic' love that makes people insist on diamonds.

The evocative nature of jewellery is often used to sell it. The absence of a piece of jewellery that has been worn daily for many years leaves the wearer with a sense of loss and, in the case of a ring, an indentation on the finger. Diamonds *are* for ever but they are often tied more closely to a sense of possession and obligation or to a sense of investment than to decoration or delight in the jewellery itself. Gloria Hickey describes gift-giving as one of the earliest forms of human material ex-change and we can assume that objects for adornment have always formed a major part of that process.

> When we give a gift we are responding to a felt obligation, or hoping to make one. This needn't be taken negatively although bribes are a good example of the shadowy aspects. The engagement ring is an equally valid, although a more acceptable form of the same behaviour.[7]

The complexity of feeling surrounding the making and wearing of jewellery is most apparent in relation to materials. Although in 1963 Graham Hughes con-fidently proclaimed the death of the idea that the intrinsic worth of jewellery resides in the value of the metal, non-precious jewellery still makes many people uneasy. It may be that we are wary of modern techno-logical miracles that fail to hold their promise. It may also be that the proliferation of materials has been so rapid that we have not had the time to develop trust in the properties, or even a familiarity with the poly-syllabic names, of the wonder materials of the late-twentieth century.

The only new material used seriously by jewellers in the first half of the twentieth century was platinum, which is a more expensive metal than gold. The problem for jewellers and consumers in the second half of the century is to cope with so many new materials that are in themselves worth virtually nothing. Some jewellers have overcome this problem by working with one material and slowly developing the possibilities of that material, producing work that has delighted and surprised. But more than a mere development of technical expertise is needed for this to be convincing.

Jane Adam has worked solely in anodised

aluminium since her final year as an undergraduate.

[My work is] very much jewellery, not metalsmithing. But I've taken a lot of the approaches of ceramics into jewellery, particularly the techniques of decoration. Like a thrower I repeat pieces but they are never identical and if you can do something on paper or cloth then you can do it on aluminium. I am interested in texture and I never apply colour to look flat, you can always see the brush strokes. Some people have thought that it's a photographic process but it's not. I'm always experimenting, always changing, and I try and do something different for each collection.

All my work is curved, curves are really important and I never do anything with straight edges because metal comes to life when you curve it. It becomes much more interesting and sits much better on the body because bodies aren't flat. You can't solder aluminium, which forces you into ingenuity. I used to make all the fittings but now I realise that it's important to spend time on the right things. When I see people spending time on things that don't matter it hurts me. All my edges are finished well, which people don't really register but they'd notice if they weren't.

It seems that there is a greater public acceptance of a variety of materials in contemporary jewellery. To achieve the spectacular colours and effects in his jewellery and metalwork Roger Doyle combines materials such as diamonds, steel, aluminium and gold in ways that challenge the orthodoxy of silversmithing and goldsmithing. He finds that the consumer, or perhaps more accurately in his case, the commissioner, welcomes the use of such varied materials.

I work mainly to commission and I've done a lot of black steel work with diamonds. I was trying to find a black process which would actually stay on and we've found it now with aluminium. I have had no problems with aluminium and people relating it to saucepans – they never say that and they never complain that it's expensive. You've got to keep moving. If you don't, then you get stagnant, you don't get any new ideas and you don't have any fun.

The combination of precious and non-precious materials in one piece of work can cause technical problems for the jeweller but also raises questions about the role of the assay offices and the use and meaning of hallmarks. Barbara Christie feels that Britain lags behind international opinion on hall-marking and believes that the time is right for a re-evaluation of hallmarking practice by taking jewellers' views into consideration.

The Dutch regulations are very different – there the jewellers themselves do the hallmarking and I believe it's the same in Germany – they make up their own materials and have the right to do so, they don't rely on the bullion dealers. This allows you to mix materials in a piece and you can call the gold component 'gold' rather than 'yellow metal'.

The search for new materials and new combinations of materials continues. Having combined diamonds and steel on her minimalist jewellery, Barbara Christie has been currently developing a new gold alloy. Scilla Speet, in conjunction with Peter Johns of Middlesex University, has worked on a new silver alloy which is a considerable improvement on past silvers. He has perfected the alloy and she has created unit-produced work to test it out. Like sterling silver, the new alloy is 92.5 percent pure silver but Johns has put in a tiny amount of germanium which is a semi-conductor. The qualities of the new alloy are remarkable. Speet says:

It works like 18-carat gold for me, so it's almost a different material from silver. It oxidises less and it needs much less annealing and you can spot-weld it, which you can't usually do with silver. At Central Saint Martins I have been working with Rosemary House from woven textiles. We have been experimenting with woven silver fabric and woven silk by spot-welding

Simon Fraser
Necklace, 1992
Flower bulbs
Made for Derek Jarman

settings on it without burning. I want to make fashion jewellery that is half-textile and half-silver, which would cut the weight down and give body to the textiles.

But materials alone do not make good jewellery. It is easy to forget the varied and specialist skills that are needed to transform materials into jewellery. As David Pye, the writer on crafts, wrote:

> In speaking of good materials we are paying unconscious tribute to the enormous strength of tradition of workmanship skill shaping the world even now (and still largely unwritten). We talk as though good materials were found instead of being made. It is good only because workmanship has made it so. Good workmanship will make something better out of pinchbeck than bad will out of gold. *Corruptio optimi pessima.* Some materials promise far more than others but only the workman can bring out that promise.[8]

Peter Hinks reminds us that it was not until the late 1960s that jewellery and silversmithing techniques really changed and developed from those used in the Renaissance. The major changes came from post-war production methods and the demands of very new materials, making the role of the technician or craftsman as important as that of the designer in the new jewellery courses, whatever the materials used. Brian Wood recognised this in his vision of the course at Central:

> ... with the decline of Hatton Garden with its craftsmen and apprentices and the streamlining of higher education the jewellery course at Central Saint Martins is one of the few places where such a variety of techniques can be learnt and such a breathtaking standard of skill achieved.[9]

The skills that are passed on to the students are the chief concern of the technicians. Some jewellers prefer to work as technicians rather than tutors and this choice usually arises from their passion for material

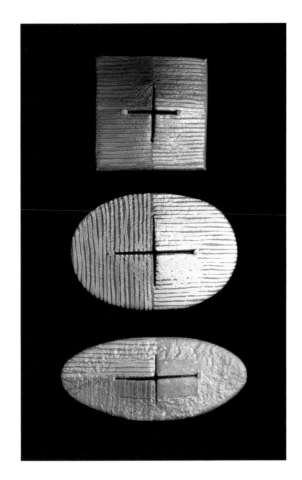

Jane Adam
Reticulated brooches, 1997
Dyed anodised aluminium

Jane Adam
Bangles, 1996
Dyed anodised aluminium

Roger Doyle
Art Deco clock, *c.*1973
Silver casing

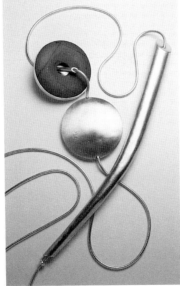

Barbara Christie
Pendant 1997
Gold and silver

and techniques. John Leech, who was a technician on the course from 1970 until 1986, describes the predicament of the technician: 'You are so busy helping other people that you no longer want to help yourself. It's difficult to do your own work when you are thinking about other people's all the time. I do admit to being a bit of a jack-of-all-trades but I do try to be a perfectionist. All I have to do is look at a problem and my brain sorts it out for me – that made being a technician the perfect job.'

Chris Howes has been a technician at Central since 1975. He served a five-year apprenticeship and worked as an engineer before specialising in jewellery in his Diploma in Art and Design at Birmingham. When describing his approach to jewellery and metalwork he emphasises the need to consider materials and techniques together:

> The work that I do is very influenced by the way I work with a material. The detailed appearance of the piece seems to be largely determined by the process I use. I'm not someone who decides upon something and then does everything necessary to create exactly that. For me working with the material will teach me as much and suggest to me how an object ought to be as much as my own aesthetic decisions. I am fascinated by techniques: I see a visual effect and I want to know how to make it. For example, patination. I started playing around with chemicals and metals and I liked the effects. Working as a technician and having to show people techniques was a good way of developing my range.

Martin Hopton came to jewellery as a mature student at the age of twenty-eight. He had trained as a cabinet maker and considered being a sculptor but decided on jewellery because it combined the three-dimensional approach to design with techniques and a sense of scale to which he responded. By the third year of his degree, he decided that jewellery was not enough for him.

I produced two watches for my final show. One was a brooch affair with a timepiece in it and it had a pendulum which didn't actually serve any purpose – it was just visually there – and one wristwatch. I think the wristwatch was the start of the work that I pursue now. I concentrate mainly on watches even though I do produce a range of jewellery, the watches are my passion – the things I've learnt to love.

I always had a little bit of a problem with jewellery for jewellery's sake. For me to make a timepiece was to make something that was a piece of jewellery, it was a piece of sculpture but it also had a function.

I've gone from designing so-called modern pieces to restoring pieces from about 1750. I can almost build a clock movement of that period now. The most complete thing for me would be to do all the case design plus the movement. It brings me into the realms of silversmithing and I think every jeweller should have a little knowledge of the techniques of silversmithing.

For Scilla Speet the exercise and development of technical knowledge and skill is one of the most rewarding aspects of the jeweller's craft. Her enthusiasm is almost utopian:

> I like the whole process of handling the materials, forming them and being pleased with the end result. I like a mechanical challenge. I like to be dictated to by the customer's challenge and I like making tools. I like quantity production, technical processes, and I specialise in hidden snaps and catches because I like the mechanics of it all.

> My father took me to Norway five times so I was very lucky. I loved the beautiful clear lines and big expanses of silver and pewter – the later Jensen stuff – clear and minimalistic forms. Everyone was re-thinking jewellery at the time, getting rid of stones and creating clean forms, clean surfaces. The Dutch jewellers such as Gies Bakker and Emmy van Leersum helped to get rid of all that pretty clutter in jewellery.

Roger Doyle
Necklace, c.1990
18-carat gold, light-green tourmalines,
carved rubellite, diamonds and enamel

Scilla Speet
Armband and earring, 1997
New silver alloy

Scilla Speet
Earring, 1997
New silver alloy

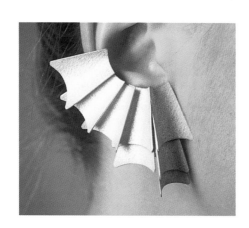

Martin Hopton
Watch, 1995
Silver casing

Chris Howes
Watch, 1995
Silver casing

Tom Scott
Sauce Boat, 1975
Silver
Made for the Drapers Company

Martin Baker
Jam and honey pots,
1995
Silver and enamel

Although the consumer may not be aware of the process in making jewellery, and may be simply entranced by the product, there is a great deal of respect for skill and craftsmanship within the jewellery community. Some, such as Margaret Turner and Martin Baker, have mastered all the techniques and the skills to bring their ideas to fruition.

Martin Baker describes himself as a small-worker, mainly making precious *objets d'art* and jewellery. 'My sources are organic, natural and figurative and I try to put some sort of quality into it that is not seen at first glance.'

Few jewellers, however, have a total command of all techniques and most are generous in their praise of others. Some feel that the maker and the designer should both be named when a piece is displayed, as proposed in the original manifesto of the Arts and Crafts Exhibition Society in 1888. However, Tom Scott is diffident about his talents: 'If I analyse it I think "What else can I do? I can't do anything else." I don't do any of my own work now. I work for Andrew Grima in Switzerland and go over a couple of times a year, which I enjoy and I have been working for Cartier doing trophies, which is limiting. Roger Doyle wrote a reference for me to become a Freeman of the Worshipful Company of Goldsmiths. He said "Tom's life is totally devoted to making jewellery. He is the only person who, on his deathbed, will say 'I should have spent more time in the workshop'."'

Leo and Ginnie de Vroomen acknowledge the team that makes the production of their ideas possible, especially the work of Gisèle Moore, another ex-Central student who designs their more commercial ranges of fine jewellery, leaving Ginnie de Vroomen to concentrate on commissions. The de Vroomens also employed Fred Rich to enamel for them early in his career. Some jewellers such as Graham Fuller have specialised in lending their talents to others:

> My talents are spread around but it's important to me to stay with this craft. I was asked by Roger Doyle to do some work. For him it's got to be 100 percent right.

I relate to his accuracy and precision. I made his Diamond International Award piece for 1996. It's nice seeing his publicity. Through him I've started doing work for John Donald again, which is lovely, his work is so different, it's a much easier style.

For the students I give more technical input than anything else. You give them any technical knowledge you can. You explain different ways of doing things and they go away and come to their own decisions and conclusions. I think that it's better for the students if they get a different person each day.

The idea of skill sharing has been taken one step further by Tom McEwan, who allows fellow jewellers to use his workshop space and has a system whereby each jeweller buys a specialist piece of equipment that can be used by all. This spirit of co-operation is reflected in jewellery education. Peter Page is an exponent of this when teaching at Central. 'Most of the teachers who come in to teach at Central, and indeed elsewhere are practising people themselves and they've got a lot to give to the students. There's a tradition in jewellery that you don't keep things to yourself – you hand them on. Having my own workshop and designing and making my own jewellery made me feel I had quite a good balance between the design side and the making side. So I was able to talk to students about their designs and how to put their designs into three dimensions.'

Page prefers to work on individual commissions rather than selling through shops. He wants to work with his customers on something that they want rather than expecting them to purchase what someone else thinks they ought to have. Page's interest in design and in technique come together in pieces such as the 50th Birthday Jewel which was commissioned by the designer Rodney Fitch.

> Three or four years ago I made a gold house for Rodney Fitch which broke up into six pieces of jewellery. That was technically quite an interesting thing to do and it took me about five months to make.

The roof and walls were enamelled, the walls in red and green, like ivy growing up the side of the house, which Jane Short did beautifully, of course.

Part of Page's technical and stylistic development took place when he went to Canada in the late 1970s. He shared a workshop with Bill Read, a North Western Coast Native Canadian. Page recalls the skills of Canadian craftsmen.

I went out in 1977 and helped teach North West Coast craftsmen. I can see it now, although I wouldn't have seen it at the time, that I've definitely been influenced by their flow of line and their drawings of eyes and animals and figures; they have been a great influence on my work. I like a clean flow of line, definitely flowing. The only person who depresses me is René Lalique. When I first saw his work I thought 'Oh golly! I'll never be as good as that.' He combined a wonderful style with superb craftsmanship.

A different and perhaps more contemporary approach to the craft of jewellery is that exemplified by Eric Spiller. He has moved from the hands-on approach to jewellery-making. He remembers the Central course as being skill-based and that the emphasis on technical ability allowed him to develop his ideas without being constrained by lack of technique. A minimalist who makes brooches, he describes his interests thus:

My interest in minimalism started at the RCA. I came from a science background, in fact I'd started a degree in organic chemistry prior to the jewellery course at Central. I was just fascinated by new technology and entranced by the sheer volume of machinery available at the RCA. I didn't use much silver or gold, I don't know why. I suppose that it was fun working in a wide range of materials. Indeed it's only in this country that I found an obsession with precious materials. Anyway, many of the production methods and techniques seemed like the wrong processes for gold and silver.

Now my research involves trying to remove the 'hands-on' component from jewellery-making. It's part of a greater debate – whether craft has to 'hand and heart', something that the Crafts Council subscribes to but to which I am less wedded. I'm now moving into digital technology and working with manufacturing firms to develop my ideas. Europe and the Far East have always been important markets for me and I sell more there than I do in Britain. I am working with a group of designers, including Gordon Burnett, on a computer-controlled design and manufacture project. My particular work provides digitised images that are translated into metal components by chemical and mechanical milling. It is a process that provides incredible control and offers the facility of work closely with the client and make 'on screen' decisions prior to production.

I keep on telling myself that I should change scale but there is a comfort factor in a scale that fits into the hand. It is really sculpture on a small scale.

He seems able to combine the use of new technology, the traditional relationship of the jeweller and client in the conception and production of a unique piece of jewellery and a feeling for jewellery as a sculptural medium. Some of his aims in making jewellery can only be achieved by machine: the precision cutting and finishing of his chosen material, anodised aluminium, creates an object of perfect minimalism. And his collaborations with companies across the globe are made possible by international computer links. What he designs in Scotland can be made elsewhere without any loss of ideas of information in the transition. The use of computer technology in jewellery design may threaten some and be irrelevant to others, but it is a reality which many jewellers will have to come to terms with in the future.

Peter Page
Necklace for Edward, 1996
18-carat gold and cabochon sapphires

Peter Page
House, 1991
18-carat gold and enamel
by Jane Short
Made for Rodney Fitch

Peter Page
House, as six pieces of
jewellery, 1991
18-carat gold and enamel
by Jane Short
Made for Rodney Fitch

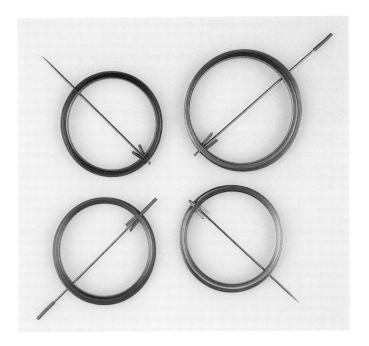

Eric Spiller
4 brooches, 1984
Anodised aluminium

Eric Spiller
4 brooches, 1996
Anodised aluminium

1　Aldous Huxley, in Graham Hughes, *The Art of Jewellery*, Studio Vista, 1972, p.239

2　David Poston, 'The medium is not the message', *Crafts*, no.68, May/June 1984, p.15

3　Isaiah Berlin, 'The idea of pluralism', in *The Fontana Post-Modern Reader*, Fontana, 1996, pp.42–8

4　David Pye, 'Design Proposes, Workmanship Disposes', in *Craft Classics since the 1940s*, Crafts Council, 1988, p.88

5　Clare Phillips, *Jewelry from Antiquity to the Present*, Thames and Hudson, 1996, p.78

6　Colette, *The Bracelet*, translated by Matthew Ward in *The Collected Short Stories of Colette*, Penguin, 1985, p.97

7　Gloria Hickey, 'Craft within a consumer society', in *The Culture of Craft*, Manchester University Press, 1997, p.84

8　David Pye, *op.cit.* p.87

9　Jane Rapley, 'Brian Wood's Obituary', in *The Independent*, 14 September 1991, p.9

Enamelling

Photograph of Patrick Furse, Stefan Knapp
and others working on enamel mural for
Alexander Supermarket, New Jersey, 1961

The high quality of enamel, as differentiating it from all other substances employed in the arts, is the great power of its unrivalled colour.[1]

The combination of technique and materials can be seen at its most breathtaking in the work of enamellers.

In the nineteenth century, John Ruskin had tried to revive the art of enamelling which had gradually diminished in importance as an art form since the Middle Ages. In 1860 he established a prize for the best piece of enamelling in the *champlevé* style. This method of applying different coloured enamels within areas defined by metal wire was the technique used by the fourteenth-century Limousin enamellers and appealed greatly to Ruskin the medievalist. It was one of the many hand techniques which he feared would disappear in the nineteenth-century world of production for the masses, if not of mass-production. Despite this encouragement and some interesting and technically challenging work done under the aegis of the Arts and Crafts Exhibition Society at the turn of the century, enamelling never gained a wide following amongst silversmiths and jewellers in the early twentieth century. One of the problems was the search for suitable subject-matter.

Ruskin preferred historical and religious themes for this work but the practitioners themselves wanted enamelling to be brought into the modern age. Alexander Fisher wrote 'The art of enamelling on metal' in 1906 when he worked at Central under the first Principal, W.R. Lethaby. The book was intended to be a textbook for schools of art and design and was based on studio practice at Central.

Enamels must never be copies of anything in nature, nor of any other process of painting in art. They should be creations. They are for the representation and embodiment of thoughts, ideas, imaginings and those parts of the world which exist only in our mind.[2]

This rather daunting dictum added to the problems of the enameller. As a technique, enamelling has always been precious because it is hard to achieve the desired effect precisely. The materials are simple: ground glass, pigment, and any metal from steel to gold, and heat is used to bond the glass to the metal. However, the possibilities for error are endless. Writing about Fred Rich in *Goldsmiths' Review 1995–96*, David Beasley describes the painstaking process of firing enamel, something that cannot be hurried or streamlined even today.

The firing varies between thirty seconds and two minutes at each time depending on the size of the piece, yet the preparation may be as much as ten hours' work. As the colours are built up, the firings and timing become more critical – they become fraught because the final firings are so critical. I use lots of different colours of different firing temperatures and because I carve the metal in relief, they are of varying thicknesses. Keeping a balance between all these criteria and pulling the thing out of the kiln at exactly the right moment can lead to a nervous breakdown.[3]

Patrick Furse
Lethaby panel, 1982
Enamel on steel

Stefan Knapp
Alexander Supermarket Mural in situ, 1962

The aesthetic constraints imposed on the enameller
and the technical challenges of the technique
combined to dissuade jewellers and metalworkers from
developing enamels in the first half of the century. In
1953 Peter Floud wrote: 'In the 1890s remarkable work
in *champlevé* and in painted enamels was being
executed by Alexander Fisher, Nelson Dawson and
others and Clement Heaton was experimenting in
cloisonné. Today practically nothing is being done,
other than by routine production of heraldic enamels
for presentation silver.'[4]

By the 1960s enamel seemed too painstaking and risky and the colours available too limited to really fire the imagination. Ros Conway recalls experimenting with enamel at college but she found it impossible to get the results that she wanted. Peter Hinks reflects on the paradox of the dearth of enamelling at a time when jewellery was becoming more colourful. It was left to the artist whose own work was at the opposite end of the scale to jewellery to develop a new and vibrant approach to enamels.

Patrick Furse was a lecturer at Central from 1970 until 1984. During that period he worked in the School of Fine Art, where he specialised in large-scale enamel murals, and in the Jewellery Department, where he expanded the range of enamel colours available.

As a student at Chelsea Polytechnic, now Chelsea College of Art and Design, the declaration of war made further study impossible. Following the war, he tried to go back to Chelsea but found it easier to work on his own. The turning point came when he met Stefan Knapp, the painter and enamellist:

I saw his first painting exhibition around the same time I went to the Central because I was interested in printmaking. I went as a part-time student working under Merlyn Evans. I did one quite elaborate colour print of four etched aquatint copper plates. It was interesting but it was immensely laborious.

Then I saw Stefan Knapp's work – I think it was his first large-size mural for St Anne's College at Oxford – three great big panels. I was very excited because of the colour. Instead of being printed off-metal, [the colour] was actually on the metal. But I didn't like to ask him how he did it. So I groped around and found some American books on it and I pieced it together gradually but I only had a Bunsen burner and it wasn't a very good way to fuse enamel and I didn't think I would get anywhere.

Stefan Knapp learned that Furse was interested in enamel and invited him to help on his large-scale mural project for the architect Frederick Gibberd at Heathrow Airport. Furse also worked with Knapp on a huge enamel mural for Alexander supermarket in New Jersey.

Knapp worked with thin layers of enamels on large sheets of metal using a technique that he had developed himself. Furse was impressed because it overcame the problem of the strident colours of pure enamels.

Stefan Knapp used pure colours but because he poured them on very thinly they skated over [the surface] and he got broken effects. Technically, it was a marvellous way of putting the enamel on thinly, that particular Abstract Expressionist way of working. He had this technique, mixing the enamel up with liquid gum and pouring it onto the panel and tilting the end. The alternative is to use an industrial enamel with a spray-gun, otherwise it distorts all over the place.

Furse's interest in enamel impressed Knapp, who recommended him to Morris Kesselman, the new Principal of Central School of Arts and Crafts, when he visited the site. Kesselman offered Furse work teaching enamelling in the Industrial Design Department and then at the Fine Art Department at Central where he started work in Autumn 1970. His kiln-building experience came in useful because he was only employed on the basis that he could provide an enamelling kiln for £5! Furse turned this into a practical lesson for his students: 'The first three or four students were each given a firebrick and told to start cutting a groove and when they'd cut a groove they were told to take a rod and wind nichrome wire around it. They were astonished. We built the furnace upstairs [at the Central site in Southampton Row] – it lasted several years.'

Although he was employed to teach mural enamelling to Fine Art students, Furse was sought out by other students, particularly jewellers. And when Brian Wood saw his mural work he formalised the arrangement by asking him to teach enamelling in the jewellery department. Furse agreed, despite reservations that he knew nothing about jewellery; he was only slightly reassured by Wood's assertion that this did not matter.

At a time when new colourful and comparatively easily-worked materials such as resins, plastics and titanium were becoming more easily available, it might seem strange to resuscitate an ancient craft such as enamelling. But the interest in new materials was accompanied by a desire to understand and master ancient techniques and, through experimentation, to bring them up to date.

This is an example of the pluralism that informed the visual arts in the 1970s and 1980s, a pluralism that allowed the rediscovery of enamels and related techniques such as *pâté de verre*, whereby a clay mould of an object is packed with grains of glass and fired. There was also a recognition that new materials were limited and that there were effects and responses to be gained from the rediscovery of past techniques. Furse's approach was exemplary:

> The first thing I had to do was to sit down and prepare colour samples. The teaching part was experimental and I wanted them to have the complete colour range; transparent and opaque, on silver and on gold so that they could see the full range of possibilities. I didn't like the strong colours of pure enamel and so I spent years and years mixing enamels and then having them finely ground and then remixed and remixed again so that I eventually made up a whole palette of my own. That was one problem, to avoid strident colours. The second problem was to get definite shapes without the old techniques, so I had to devise my own ways.

Jane Short, who was a student on the jewellery course from 1972 to 1975, recollects Furse's methods.

> Pat set up a very thorough little system for us to work within. He set out the nuts and bolts of colour and little test pieces. He made it easy to find out about the subject. It's one of those subjects that can bamboozle people. If you don't get help you can spend a lot of time doing something not very nice and get discouraged so it

was good to have it all set up. If you can't see what the colours are you can't respond to them. When you don't know what's available to you then you are working in a blind corner. Pat didn't have so much to do with what you did with the enamel, although I must have had conversations with him about this. At that time he wasn't a jewellery enameller, he was a large-scale panel enameller and he was still finding things out himself. He had a very thorough attitude, which was useful to me.

The problems of creating large-scale enamel panels preoccupied Patrick Furse throughout his working life. He wanted to devise a method of working which did not require a large furnace in his studio and hoped that this would provide a paradigm of working practice for other enamellers.

> I created my own process. I bolted one panel face-to-face with another panel, using strips so that they would not touch and carried them on a bus to Central and then brought them back. It was to prove that you could work on any site without a furnace. I used to go to a factory in North London and they let me do my firing during the change-over period between the day shift and the evening shift. There were forty-five minutes when the furnace was doing nothing and there was somebody on duty. I'd fire them and then bring them back to Central to do the next coat and return with them a few days later. It's a long way from a Bunsen burner to a twenty-foot furnace.

Patrick Furse finally stopped working with large-scale enamels because of the huge amount of effort involved. Subsequently he trained as an engraver at Sir John Cass College in London, and he now engraves jewellery made by his wife, Antonia. He has also returned to his first artistic interest, painting.

For Jane Short, the discovery of enamelling gave her work focus and direction.

> If I'd been to a different course I may or may not have

Clive Burr
Clock for
Jaeger le Coultre, 1994
Atmospheric movement,
glass, silver gilt and
enamel by Jane Short

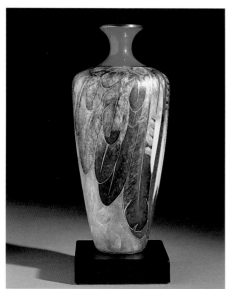

Jane Short
Bird Vase, 1990 (view 1)
Enamel on silver

Jane Short
Bird Vase, 1990 (view 2)
Enamel on silver

been exposed to enamelling and there may or may not have been someone to help me. For me it was crucial because it was where I discovered the thing I seem to be best at. It was like a love affair and it's an inward thing. If enamel was a person then I would definitely be very much in love with him. I see my work as a dialogue between me and the technique. I happened to use very thin wire within the enamel and that dictated the way it looked for quite a long time until I got to the point where I thought I knew exactly what I could do with this technique. So, because I'm interested in not knowing what's going to happen – the discovery of the new – I started to do more engraving from about 1987 onwards. I've been doing a lot of engraving under the enamel and it's got quite florid and rich.

Engraving's a very deliberate technique. It looks like a person has made this mark. It's not like etching which has a less direct look, or like patination. It's difficult sometimes to make it look unmanufactured. I'm also engraving the metal back and enamelling but then also texturing the surrounding metal. I used to cover the metal completely with enamel but now sometimes I let the metal do things. It is like a dialogue and a constant investigation because once you lose the spirit of 'what's going to happen, and can I do this?' and enjoying it, then it is difficult to maintain the integrity of the piece.

Jane Short has tried to communicate this enthusiasm for the technique and the need for an experimental attitude through teaching as well as through her own work. Brian Wood approached her after her MA show and invited her to return to Central as a tutor. She has also taught in other art and design colleges across the world and her teaching skills have allowed others to share her skill and passion for enamel.

Her work has developed and changed as her own circumstances have changed. As well as developing her work through technical challenges she uses her surroundings and events in her life to develop her style. Wherever she is and whatever she does her experiences feed in to her work. In 1979 she won a travel bursary from the RCA and she chose to travel to Japan since she was influenced generally by Japanese art and design.

In commissioned work, which forms the greater part of her silversmithing practice, Short is restricted by her clients' wishes but in her own work she makes the personal into art. Some of this work is unashamedly autobiographical and she intends to continue in this vein.

When I had my first child I found it very difficult to think about anything other than babies. Not that I'm particularly keen on babies but it is such a change to your life especially if you've waited until your late thirties to do it. It's a real shock to the system and so if I sat down to do any work I could only think about babies. So I did work that had children and babies in it, quite figurative work. I did one of my son in a little sun and I was waiting for him to come out. I've done one of him as an angel, which he isn't and he is; whether other people think that is what it's about is another question.

Fred Rich was among the students taught enamelling by Jane Short. He was an exceptional student who became as obsessed as she was with enamels. Patrick Furse remembers him as 'very adventurous, he was extraordinary from the very beginning'. Like Jane Short, Rich left the jewellery course at Central and has concentrated on silversmithing and enamelling. Unlike Short he has not been content to remain working within the traditional small scale of enamelling and has specialised in creating large enamelled silver pieces and is constantly trying to push the medium further in terms of scale and technical content.

Rich took to enamelling with enthusiasm. He was obsessed with colour and Patrick Furse's highly developed palette of enamel colours allowed him to achieve 'bright, bright colour: the only way you're going to get it is through enamel. What I remember about my degree show is Brian saying that I had to get the shapes sorted out and I was thinking "Well it's not about shape at the moment, bugger the shape, that can come later and I still think that now".'

After his degree he worked on his own and then shared a workshop with Tom McEwan and Annabel Eley, eventually deciding that he preferred working alone at home. His work includes enamelling for such jewellers as Leo and Ginnie de Vroomen, Roger Doyle and Stephen Webster but most of his energy goes into one-off pieces of his own devising. These are rarely commissions because his unique relationship with Garrards means that he is in the enviable position of being able to make work entirely as he wishes. Fred Rich recollects the start of his relationship with Garrards when he was asked to create a piece for Garrards's 1993 exhibition *Royal Plate of the Twentieth Century.*

Basically it was an historical exhibition of silver throughout the century and as part of the exhibition they asked various contemporary silversmiths to submit designs that could be bought, carrying on that tradition of patronage. I put in a small enamel beaker which I'd been thinking about for ages. It got a lot of attention from all sorts of people, which was very good – anyway it was a start. They sold the piece twice over so I had to remake it.

[Garrards] really liked this piece so they asked me to design some other things which they sold. Richard Jarvis, one of the directors of Garrards, organised an exhibition of my work, all silver and enamel. The agreement was that I was going to do work for about a year-and-a-half and they would buy the pieces from me and keep them and put the exhibition on, which we just about managed by the skin of our teeth.

The one-man show at Garrards, in October 1995, was a success; all the work was sold. They now plan to hold another solo exhibition of Rich's work in 1999. Their exceptional support has allowed him to develop his enamelling techniques together with a personal iconography:

There's a technique I have been developing, bringing all the things I've been interested in together. Basically it's *cloisonné* enamel but it's all soldered and then it's all carved, so you have got *cloisonné*, enamel and relief carving, it works really well. When it comes to soldering wire on, you do it as if you were drawing. Obviously you can't just draw wire on but the way you do it is the same movement and the same attitude. You get a spontaneous feel to it and all the different disciplines come together. Its all quite naturalistic and gives a feeling of richness. I just like things to be absolutely saturated. It isn't that far from gaudy – it's just this side of taste! I think an emotional response to my work is important. You either love it or hate it. I don't mind people hating the work but I don't like people criticising it unknowledgeably.

Although Ros Conway was attracted to enamelling when she was a student at Central from 1970 to 1973 she found it difficult to get involved with it and did not enjoy the work that she did. This she later remedied when she received a Crafts Council grant to study with Jane Short for two years in the 1980s. The work she made in this period went into a one-woman show at the Victoria and Albert Museum in 1982.

Perhaps the most important element in her enamel work was her collaboration with the painter Hughie O'Donnell. They admired each other's work in their different chosen media. O'Donnell approached her to jewel his paintings and she immediately saw how well their work would go together. It sounds too pedestrian to explain that she made pieces that he painted and then the two were exhibited together but that in essence was what happened in the Marlborough Gallery, London in 1989. Most of the pieces were sold (painting and jewellery together). Although this was exciting and Conway felt that she had at last 'got the point of enamel', she wanted to take the technique further.

When a metal form is covered with enamel it often looks as though it is made of glass and this is the aspect of enamel that Conway wanted to develop. She

Leo and Ginnie de Vroomen
Brooch, 1989
Platinum, diamonds and enamel
by Fred Rich

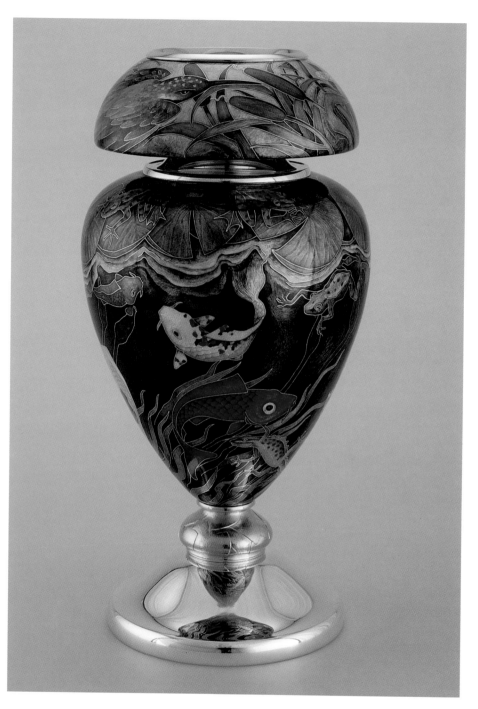

Fred Rich
Kingfisher Vase, 1996
Gold, silver and enamel
Won the Jacques Cartier Award

contacted a former jeweller called Diana Hobson who was working with the technique called *pâté de verre*: 'It's a technique that was developed in the last century in France and that has been revived by Diana Hobson. You make a clay mould of an object and pack the interior of the mould with grains of glass, like in enamelling. This you fire, which takes a long time, like a ceramic. You then take the mould away and you are left with the piece – hopefully. It's extremely difficult to get right.'

Despite the technical challenges Conway has fallen under the spell of this extraordinary light and fragile, glowing glass:

> It's going to be glass from now on. I've taken a long time to get round to it but it gives me more pleasure than anything else. I may try to mix all my skills together. I think that I may electro-form in silver some of the moulds I have made for glass and enamel them too – I just want lots more time.

As well as her own work, Conway now teaches glass for jewellers, which includes enamelling, at Middlesex University. Like Jane Short and others, Conway passes down the difficult but rewarding techniques of enamel ensuring that they are unlikely to be lost to future generations of jewellers and silversmiths.

Tom McEwan was attracted to the colour possibilities of enamel and feels that the technique gave him a direction for his design work. He still uses a great deal of colour but now prefers stones to enamel. Like Fred Rich, Fiona Rae, who was taught by Jane Short, became interested in enamel as an extension of her interest in colour but unlike Rich she was as interested in sculpture as painting.

> Because I was coming at it with a very strong interest in painting and not being quite sure whether jewellery was right for me, it was like a Godsend when I discovered enamel and I could combine the two approaches. It allowed me to discover metals as well and there are inherent qualities in metal that I enjoy working with.

The enamels Rae made when she was a student showed a remarkable subtlety and restraint in colouring. She devised flower forms that had matt enamel in graduated colour and thus further developed the repertoire of the enamellist. She now teaches enamelling at Central and makes commissioned work as well as repairing articles such as an enamelled church plate from the first flowering of the Arts and Crafts movement a hundred years ago.

Whereas Rae is interested in developing her use of materials and her work with colour, Giles Last is more concerned with the purpose and context of his enamels.

> I like site-specific art work – which jewellery tends to be. You're designing for a specific part of someone's body or someone's persona or someone's table. I was taught some enamelling at Leamington Spa by Rosemary Zencon and Tammy de Winter. At an early stage it felt familiar and I enjoyed the colour and the process and the high craft of it.

For Giles Last, the boundaries between art, craft and design are made meaningless by enamel. He has also moved his work from the confines of formal education into the community.

When Last graduated he started working for a project which had been set to teach enamelling to people with disabilities in Deptford, South London. The project had been running successfully for several years. The project showed the versatility of enamel: it can be used by the inexperienced to create worthwhile work relatively simply. Its alchemical process transforms the base into something shining and colourful.

> I enjoy working with people as well as being closed off in a studio and I gain quite a lot of my inspiration from everyday life, personal histories and the world around me. That sort of thing I find does transfer very clearly into visual shapes and forms. I've always enjoyed working with different types of community, not necessarily

art schools. The closer you get to the community you live in the more interesting it gets, so I do like social history and the people side of things.

Last also worked rather less happily in adult education where the numbers were too large to teach properly and he worked for Dinny Hall until 1990 when he moved to Barcelona. The move was prompted by a visit to the Exposition Biennale at Limoges in 1988 where he had seen the vibrant and exciting enamels produced in Catalonia.

He worked with enamellers in Barcelona and was allowed to use equipment in the art school. Here he found that there was no distinction between craft and art, and enamellers worked in all formats, from miniatures to large panels, and different ways of working were often combined. There was also a different technical tradition to the one at Central: cold enamel painting. This included the use of *grisaille*: opalescent colours built up in layers to give an illusion of form, an illusion of three dimensions in two dimensions. His relationship with his peers in Barcelona was reciprocal and he helped them to develop their *cloisonné* techniques.

Enamel is a particularly difficult technique, whether applied to silversmithing or jewellery. There are still no quick and easy ways of practising this technique. It might appear to be out of tune with the times in which we live and yet it provides possibilities of light and colour on metal which are impossible to create in any other way. As Jane Short says:

> ... It's certainly a perverse medium. When students are interested you are afraid to tell them all the ins and outs because you'll put them off and if you don't tell them it doesn't work and that puts them off too. But I do see interesting work being done. I'm part of the first generation of crafts people who have learned enamelling in a non-traditional way and we are now established enough to be teaching it and I think that's having an effect.[5]

1 Alexander Fisher, 'The art of enamelling upon metal', *The Studio*, 1906, p.36

2 *Ibid.* p.36

3 David Beasley, *Goldsmiths' Review 1995–96*, Worshipful Company of Goldsmiths, 1996, p.38

4 Peter Floud, 'The crafts then and now', in *Craft Classics since the 1940s*, Crafts Council, 1988, p.52

5 Jane Short quoted in Rosemary Hill, 'Coating of many colours', *Crafts*, no.68, May/June 1984, p.30

Ros Conway
Form, 1997
Pâté de verre

Ros Conway
Jewel, 1983
Silver and enamel
Part of collaborative work with Hughie O'Donnell

Giles Last
Panel, 1996
Enamel on steel

Giles Last
Ring, 1995
Silver and enamel

Fiona Rae
Cufflinks, 1997
Silver and enamel

Fiona Rae
Earrings, 1996
18-carat gold, enamel and aquamarine

Beyond Jewellery

Susanna Heron and David Ward
Light projection, 1979

The new generation emerging in the 1960s and 1970s questioned the nature of jewellery and its role in society and, as in other art forms, accepted conventions were pushed aside. Many of the most talented graduates rejected what they considered to be status-laden jewellery bound by sexual stereotypes or contaminated by exploitation in favour of the new equality conveyed by materials of almost no intrinsic worth. The boundaries where jewellery approaches sculpture, clothing or even performance were explored, and it became a medium for artistic experiment rather than simple adornment.[1]

Rosalind Krauss in 'Sculpture in the expanded field' reflects on the changes in sculpture between 1969 and 1979. She discusses the way traditional artistic disciplines have been 'kneaded and stretched and twisted in an extraordinary demonstration of elasticity, a display of the way that a cultural term can be extended to cover just about anything'. This is perhaps nowhere more true than in jewellery-making. Indeed the radical shift in the work of some jewellers, including those discussed in this chapter, could not have happened without the specific cultural conditions of postmodernism, as Krauss explains: 'For, within the situation of postmodernism, practice is not defined in relation to a given medium – sculpture – but rather in relation to the logical operations on a set of cultural terms, for which any medium – photography, books, lines on walls, mirrors, or sculpture itself might be used.'[2]

To this list we can certainly add jewellery. There is another factor in the relationship between jewellery and sculpture. Many of the people interviewed for this book cited an interest in sculpture as their reason for going into jewellery. Jewellery allowed them to develop ideas and work on a small scale and with a precision that perhaps seemed unfashionable in sculpture at the time. Some have been very successful in combining art, design and craft. Wendy Ramshaw, for example has, in her ring sets, created a series of small-scale sculptures. Peter Dormer writes: 'The directness of Wendy Ramshaw's invention for the view of jewellery

Peter Lyon
Sculpture fountain, 1980–1
Made for the Cambridge University Engineering Department

as an art off the body has not been bettered.'[3]

However, jewellers with an interest in the fine arts should not be thought of as artists manqué. Some, like Peter Lyon, have developed dual practices, working as sculptors and as jewellers, and artists such as Alexander Calder have also contributed a great deal to jewellery design. It is perhaps a failing of our perception as a society that we demand specialisation, and that we demand an easily digested or at least an easily recognised visual culture where transparency is paramount and this is most easily achieved by a clear demarcation of roles. The painter Patrick Heron is unusual in regarding the notion that artists can turn their hands to anything as ridiculous, and he refused the invitation to create jewellery for the 1961 International Jewellery Exhibition at Goldsmiths Hall. But others welcome the possibilities of this cross-fertilisation.

The dialectic between the uniqueness of artistic production and the reproducibility of design is a comparatively easy one for jewellers to deal with because the practice of most jewellers includes the unique, the one-off, usually commissioned piece, which is never reproduced. Jewellery made on production lines is usually a watered-down or simplified version of the most individual stylistic elements of the jeweller's work. The techniques of jewellery-making include those of the handworker and of the factory. Procedures such as casting, lathe-turning as well as careful hand-polishing, stone-setting and enamelling mean that the jeweller's position is pivotal.

All the practices, techniques and all of the art and design ideas can potentially be encompassed by the jeweller. This makes the creation of jewellery intensely satisfying for many of its practitioners. It also means that jewellers have at their disposal an extremely wide range of transferable skills and a spectrum of ideas. Naturally, the quality of teaching is a determining factor in the level of knowledge and ability that a jeweller can bring to his or her work. Emma Paolozzi maintains that the level of technical knowledge she gained at Central enabled her to tackle any conceptual idea that she wanted to explore.

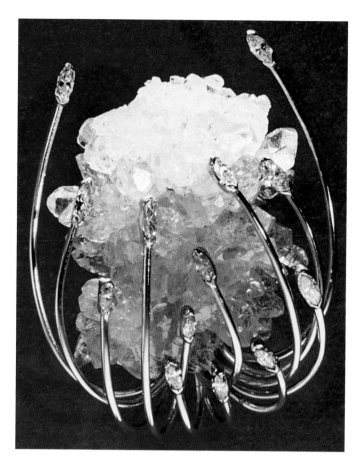

Gilian Packard
Brooch, 1964
18-carat gold, diamonds and rose quartz
Made for the Diamond International Award, 1964

Gilian Packard
Interlocking wedding and engagement rings, *c.* 1968
18-carat gold, diamonds and turquoise

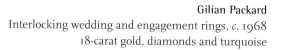

To use Krauss's model, jewellery exists in the post-modern era in the expanded field. It is not in an either/or situation: a piece of work is either jewellery or it is something else, such as sculpture. Jewellery can be jewellery in one or more of its traditional senses, it can be sculpture or part of sculpture or it can be jewellery and performance. If we take the case of ex-Central jewellery students where many of whom seemed to have moved completely into the area of sculpture, the close, almost symbiotic relationship between jewellery and sculpture can be clearly observed. This relationship is manifest in Wendy Ramshaw's ring sets, Susanna Heron's landscape sculpture or Caroline Broadhead's textile sculptures and performance work. It is also of particular acuity when considering the relationship between the body and art.

Although the relationship between jewellery and sculpture is traditional and recognised as important, it was also often dismissed as inevitable and therefore not worthy of further examination. This changed following a re-evaluation in the 1960s and 1970s when the body became an important focus of interest in art. The new jewellery course at Central was an ideal place for the development of these ideas which were fostered by staff members such as Gilian Packard.

Gilian Packard became involved with the World Crafts Council in 1964. In 1968 she became chairperson of the British sector of that organisation and in 1971 the first woman to be made a Freeman of the Worshipful Company of Goldsmiths. Her overseas connections enabled her to bring international artists into the country for lectures and exhibitions and in 1972 she brought the radical jewellers Gies Bakker and Emmy van Leersum to Britain. Their work was shown in an exhibition called *Aspects of Jewellery* in Aberdeen and they gave a lecture at the RCA which was attended by many Central students. Packard remembers that 'It was quite seminal as far as jewellery in England was concerned because the kind of people who were students here at the time were Susanna Heron, Gunilla Treen, Georgina Follett, Nuala Jamison and Caroline Broadhead. They were all people who were

very influential in jewellery and the Crafts Council took them up.'

According to Ralph Turner, experimental jewellery in the early 1970s was dominated by Bakker and van Leersum's innovative approach to jewellery and in particular by the relationship between jewellery and the body.

> Breaking with jewellery's past traditions, they waged an onslaught against elitism and orthodoxy, making a disruptive uncompromising protest with large collars and bracelets in aluminium – a light, strong, malleable and cheap material. The choice was a deliberate social, aesthetic decision. The new democratic thinking with its principles of minimal form devoid of embellishment, only became fully integrated when worn. Moreover, the body itself was considered part of jewellery and not just its setting.[4]

This new consideration of the role of the body manifested itself in such pieces as Bakker's *Invisible Jewellery* 1973, where a tight gold armlet is placed on the upper arm, it is almost invisible and when the jewellery is removed, the ghost of the armlet remains. Other noteworthy pieces were their *Body Suggestions* 1970, by which objects were placed under tight-fitting garments to change the contours of the body in mysterious ways. Although these works relate directly to the discourse of jewellery they were made during a period in which body modification for fashionable ends was beginning to be commonplace. Like most effective body-art these pieces work best as an oblique but powerful commentary on what Rudofsky calls 'the unfashionable human body'.[5]

For jewellers at the time these works redefined the possibilities of their discipline. Caroline Broadhead recalls her reaction to these ideas:

> I remember Wendy Ramshaw coming in and showing us her paper jewellery and I remember Gies Bakker and Emmy van Leersum .... I remember him coming round, looking at my work and saying 'Why aren't you

making that thing out of barbed wire?' He was very brusque and very radical at the time and I thought he was really stupid but actually that's the thing that has stuck in my mind and he was quite right. The thing that I was trying to do was in twisted silver wire with moonstones in it when in fact there was probably more of a connection with barbed wire.

Wendy Ramshaw became associated with Central in 1969 as a post-graduate student. She came to jewellery in a rather roundabout manner. At art college in Newcastle upon Tyne she was told to design and make some cutlery:

In the course of that I saw my first mill and I put pennies through and elongated the head of Queen Victoria and wore them as earrings. So I made seven pairs of huge earrings for myself for the seven days of the week – it was entirely personal.

At Reading University in the early-1960s, she noticed the quality of the surface of the etching plates and decided to cut some up into small pieces, drilled holes in them and created a range of earrings, in this case literally made out of art. She remembers Brian Wood commenting that she could make jewellery out of anything, which was what she subsequently tried to do.

The lathe was a silent object in a room. I wanted to make things in silver on it but I was told that the metal was too soft. I had a go and it worked. Nobody else did what I did on the lathe because everyone thought that I was relatively mad. Then I was successful and used it for gold. Brian Wood told me to go to the Goldsmiths Company and show my work to Graham Hughes – I didn't realise how unique those things were at the time – he bought three pieces from me that very day.

I'm in the last third of my career now and I realise that there isn't a thing that isn't useful to you, including your mistakes.

Despite the [often mentioned] sculptural nature of Ramshaw's work she still feels that design and function are as important. Ramshaw describes her current projects:

The commissions that I now get are site-specific. I'm not really a sculptor and I don't even intend to be one. There is a point in making large objects for me, if they've got a function. For example, the most exciting commission that I've got is a pair of huge swans for the V&A Museum. They are three metres by three metres each, using mild steel 4 cm thick. They are being sunk into the floor of the staff restaurant. These things will look like giant drawings coming out of the floor. I'm cutting the steel using jets of water, which is tremendously powerful and expensive. If you look back at my catalogue for my 1970 exhibition at the Pace Gallery with the things that I made at Central school in it you will see that objects were photographed against landscape: Sunderland, Hampstead Heath. Although I'd originally seen the things as small, they have their own internal scale, they can be any size.

After experimenting with different materials and approaches to jewellery, Caroline Broadhead has moved decisively into the realms of art and into textile art in particular. Her work is still centred around the body and movement and she has gradually moved into performance: for example, her 1997 designs for a dance piece called *The Waiting Game* was choreographed by Angela Woodhouse and performed at Upnor Castle in Kent. In this dance meditation that centres on waiting, anxiety and change, the costumes do not simply clothe the dancers. Rather, the wearing, exchange and re-arrangement of the garments are intrinsic parts of the piece. She started moving in this direction in the late 1970s. 'In 1976 I was also changing the direction of my work from the relatively arduous task of carving ivory to the spontanaeity and speed of working with cotton thread using flexible materials to cover or contain parts of the body. This has led me more recently to explore the interface between jewellery and clothing.'

Wendy Ramshaw
Pillar ring, 1968–9
Silver and enamel, set with amethyst

Wendy Ramshaw
Pillar ring with two side rings, 1969
Turned and enamelled silver set with two pale amethysts

Caroline Broadhead
Unlaced Grace, 1995
Dance performance
at Mills Art Centre
Banbury, Oxfordshire;
a collaboration with
Claire Russ

The metamorphosis of Broadhead's work from fashion to art was not easy. In 1991 Deborah Norton, writing in *Crafts* magazine commented on the prejudice that Broadhead faced as she developed her work into sculptural forms.

Norton questions Broadhead's impetus behind switching from jewellery to clothing and whether she sought to make serious art that is more closely linked with fashion than jewellery, in order to challenge the prevailing attitude that the art world couldn't take jewellery seriously because of its associations with fashion.[6] 'I'm pleased that my work is treading ground that makes people uneasy. I do get angry with the concept that jewellery is a frivolous thing, having to do with women and department stores, which the art world doesn't take seriously.'[7]

Broadhead found that textiles were a medium that were more responsive to her ideas than the materials traditionally associated with jewellery. But this approach had pitfalls, clothing that was not meant to be worn created resistance with some viewers. And some critics felt that Broadhead should simply design costumes. But this would not have allowed her to develop the poignant and expressive garments that stand alone, without a body for support.

In *Seven Ages*, a collection of seven individual white garments made of diverse materials (cotton, silk, nylon lace, linen and wool) she explored the relationship between clothes and the human condition:

> My interest in clothing is because of its closeness to the human being but without being a portrait or a study or anything literal.[8]
>
> In a way I'm still riveted to the figure. I like working with movement and I'm really intrigued by what someone can move in.

Some of her works defy notions of wearability, however:

> They started off as wearable garments but actually were garments that were a form of expression when they weren't being worn. It's hard to explain. After a while it seemed irrelevant that they needed to be worn. So there are quite a lot that were just art. They had the possibility of being worn because they had the right proportions and you could see that they were 'a garment'. Now they're still garments but actually very little ones and they're not about wearing anymore. They're about shadows. The latest piece that I've been doing is a little garment, a kind of miniature garment, actually it's nothing to do with the garment anymore, it's about the shadow that it casts and yet because it's a garment in the form of a person then you know what it's about. There is a subject matter. I never know where the work is going. I've always been working in the dark. If I knew where it was going it would be really boring and maybe there wouldn't be a need to make it.

Caroline Broadhead won the Jerwood Prize for Textiles in September 1997.

Susanna Heron started making jewellery in evening classes while she was still at school. With the help of her teacher, Breon O'Casey, she found a ready market for her work at the Arnolfini Gallery in Bristol, the Bear Lane Gallery in Oxford, and in 1966, Graham Hughes started buying her work for the Worshipful Company of Goldsmiths collection. She did not enjoy her time at college and spent most of her final year working at home. The staff had enough confidence in her to let her do this and to her surprise she was awarded a First for her silver and resin jewellery.

The qualities of colour and light that attracted her to resin were part of an enduring preoccupation with transparency and movement around a plane like the relationship of a bracelet to the body and the way it articulates space as the body moves. A key piece for her is the costume she made after seeing Oskar Schlemmer's work in the Bauhaus exhibition of 1969. It was partly inspired by Schlemmer's *Slatdance* design of 1922. The project was to design a piece of jewellery for a lifesize photograph and it appeared to use the space around the body, although it could only be seen from the front, there was no back, it was an illusion

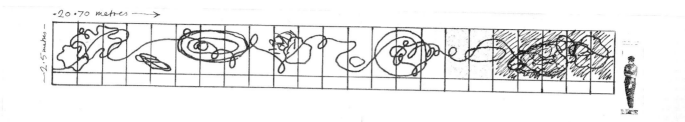

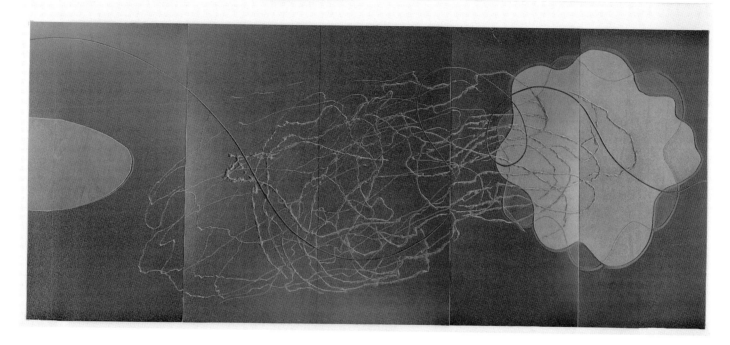

Susanna Heron
Frieze for the European Union in Brussels, 1996
Slate

Susanna Heron
Wearable, 1981
Cotton and wire frame

Susanna Heron
Neck Curve, 1979–80
Acrylic and paint

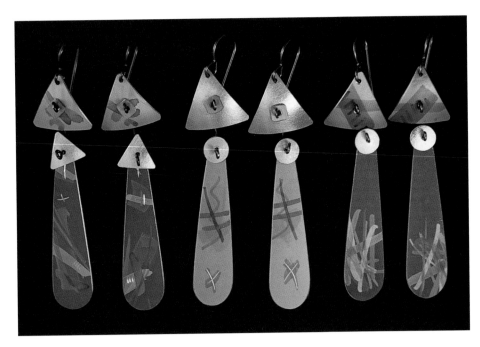

Gunilla Treen
Earrings, 1996
Anodised aluminium, silver and niobium

Gunilla Treen
I had a rest from jewellery for a number of years and I did all kind of things, such as designing scarves. But I have returned to jewellery and my preoccupations are the same: colour and materials. I want all my work to be glowing with as much colour as possible.

Julia Manheim
Yellow venetian blind backpiece, 1983
Plastic and PVC

Julia Manheim
Roll It, 1990
Painted paper and card

created for the camera.

Heron's career as a jeweller was very successful. The Electrum Gallery opened in the same month as her degree show and exhibited her work. Despite this early fame she became dissatisfied with the restrictions of jewellery-making.

> You might call jewellery a craft – but I'm not sure it is a useful term – for me, jewellery is something that is defined by use and not materials, unlike ceramics or glass. Therefore if you take the use away you end up with a useless object. The differences between jewellery and sculpture seemed more important than making an amalgam, rather than trying to make a hybrid it seems more valuable that the different areas are separate.

The Jewellery Project was commissioned by American collectors, the Knapp family, who allowed Heron and the artist and photographer David Ward to buy jewellery they thought was interesting and to curate an exhibition of this work. They designed the exhibition so that the jewellery was on tables not in cases, the only security fixings being nylon threads to fasten the work to the tables.

There were ideas connected with jewellery that Heron still found important to her work: the body moving in space, the relationship between scale and form and the movement between planes. David Ward explains these ideas in the catalogue introduction:

> Thus the human body emerges as the fundamental key to the scale and size of the works. Once this is established, then the objects tend to be conceived in relation to the body and not separately from it. The interaction of objects with the wearer is the visual point which means that the traditional interest in fine detail and technical intricacy loses its relevance. This, together with the emancipation from the use of precious materials, means that altogether new dimensions and stuctures become possible.[9]

Looking at the jewellery collected in the exhibition catalogue, one is struck by the photographs. It is an eloquent collection of ideas and images about jewellery and the body at a moment in time, rather than an exhibition of jewellery.

Writing in *Crafts* magazine, Rose Slivka discusses the approach or sense of the body as shown in the work of British jewellers in the 1980s.

> Where precious jewellery fitted the body of the wearer, now the wearer must fit – demonstrate commitment – to the piece; where before it was decorative, here it is declamatory. The wearer makes the conscious decision to the social, political and aesthetic environment for the piece. The new jewellery does not accommodate the body – rather it is in orbit around the body ... jewellery is now a body cage and a mind opener .... In the politics of magic the new English artist-jewellers are revolutionaries.[10]

But this revolution was at a time of great artistic insecurity as well as at a time of possibility. One sees this new approach to the body and jewellery manifested in the work of jewellers such as Pierre Degen, who was a technician at Central in the early 1970s. *Personal Environment* 1982, for example, is a wood and textile piece which the wearer carries over the shoulders. It is a piece of sculpture, of environmental art which can only create a tension between the body and the object, setting them as it were in opposition to each other. It speaks of the problems of adding and wearing objects on the body rather than an enhancement of the senses.

This exploration of what are best described as ideas about jewellery has not found favour with all commentators. Barbara Cartlidge's Electrum Gallery in London has celebrated the art of jewellery since 1972 but she dismisses the blurring of the distinctions between art and jewellery:

> What isn't right is to purely describe as *jewellery* what you could perhaps best, if you needed to categorise it, put into the area of *installation*. It is about as far

removed from jewellery as you can get ... it is a statement from an artist but it does not actually do anything for jewellery or people's understanding of jewellery because it is out of proportion, non-functional. ... One of the interesting facts about jewellery as an art form is that it demands to express within the limits of dimension something that is tactile, functional, emotionally felt, intellectually understandable, and, if you like, even shocking.[11]

The relationship of the body to its environment, whether that environment is on the small scale of jewellery or on the larger scale of architecture, has been a recurring theme in the work of many artists in the latter part of the twentieth century. For Susanna Heron there is always an added perspective of subjectivity. 'I'm still interested in *you* (the wearer) occupying space and in giving people an experience that is first hand; in work with which you have a direct and personal contact.'

Some of her work during this interim period related very closely to jewellery, clothing and consciousness of the body. Heron cast the interiors of bracelets to re-create the arm and then created pieces such as *Centre*, 1984: which comprised three objects based around the head and shoulders. The objects are pieces of apparel but they are unwearable; a ruff that has the centre closed, a turban that is rolled up from the middle to form a solid and a collar that has been closed.

The perplexing idea of recognisable objects that do not perform their function, that are deliberately created to deny function, is deliberately removed from Heron's previous practice of jewellery.

She has moved into making environmental art and this change also has a personal basis. After a disastrous frost in 1987 she became involved in regenerating a garden, Eagle's Nest, in Cornwall where she had grown up. From this project she created a book of photographs and words entitled *Shima: Island and Garden*, reflecting her relationship with the garden and its importance in her life.

Her subsequent work includes a long slate frieze for the new council building for the E.U. in Brussels. The frieze cannot be seen from one vantage point and the viewer is compelled to move and to look at it from different angles to appreciate it. As with her jewellery, Heron makes the viewer acutely conscious of the position of the body *vis-à-vis* the object. Her most recent works include *Sunken Courtyard* outside a community college library in East London. Here the viewer must participate by looking over the edge into the intensely blue court or out through the library windows. In 1996 she also created an environmental work of water and stone for the garden of the new British Embassy in Dublin. In all these works a high degree of participation is demanded of the viewer as they investigate the environments that Heron has created.

When Julia Manheim was a jewellery student she found the life-drawing classes the most interesting part of the course. They were given by the ceramic artist Eileen Nesbit and not fully appreciated by other students. Now, as a teacher she finds the same reluctance amongst some of her own students but she considers life drawing to be one of the most useful ways of developing ideas and a personal vision as well as providing a much needed study of the body.

Her interest in life drawing is shown in her wire-work body pieces of the early 1980s. Such pieces as *Crouching Figure* and *Ladder Neckpiece*, 1983 show her preoccupation with the line and the body. She was also producing batches of perspex jewellery at this time but her explorations into body sculpture were more important. As a resident at the then Newcastle Polytechnic sponsored by Northern Arts, she was allowed her own workshop to enable her to experiment. She stayed there for three-and-a-half years and helped to set up a designer-craftsmen course, so it is perhaps ironic that she developed her work away from the traditional confines of jewellery during this period.

I had a huge show at Sunderland, which toured to the Craft Council Galleries in London. There were a lot of plastic-coated wire pieces, pieces in plastic tubing and

Julia Manheim
Ad Hoc Art Works, 1997
Mixed media

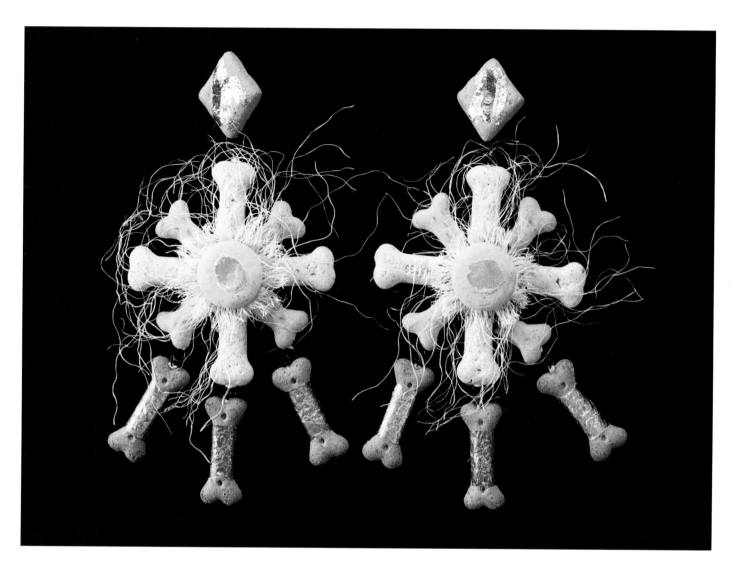

Simon Fraser
Earrings, 1989
Dog biscuits and nylon

PVC. There were body pieces and also mass-production neckpieces. I felt that I needed to make these in order to keep the other thing going. For that show, I made enormous wire human bodies, they were like drawings and they led me on to make things that weren't to be worn.

Many of the objects made 'not to be worn' were a complete departure from any notion of jewellery. Manheim started working in paper, making vessel forms but having developed a new material she returned to jewellery. 'I was making very large pieces of jewellery that went from the elbow to the wrist, for example. They were very flamboyant but were quite subtly painted. Then the objects took over and became very large and free-standing and they weren't vessel containers any more.'

But although her work was treated with interest, she found that the transition from jewellery to fine art or so-called studio-craft practice was not easy:

> It was a very difficult situation because people know you for what you have done and that can be awkward when they don't accept that you are doing something else. People still don't. I kept still being asked to be in jewellery exhibitions and that was quite nice because I could pick and choose. For example, I made some hand-held objects for a Valentine's exhibition at the V&A three or four years ago and that was a really nice thing to do because they didn't have to be worn – just picked up. They were all made from pictures from old seed catalogues because I thought it was a really nice thing giving someone flowers – only you were giving them an object made out of flowers. I've been a consultant artist on the Braintree Library Project in Essex and I'm doing one of the projects myself. The building is a sensitive site architecturally and it's circular with a big dome. I've made these really huge cast metal insets for the pavement outside the building. They are pattern cut and then cast in a foundry at Braintree, a bit like a man-hole cover. All these metal slabs are based on local history, so there are themes like

the textile industry and silk weaving and on figures such as the artist Edward Bawden, who lived in Saffron Walden, and there is one to do with straw plaiting and one with Roman pottery and one on John Rae, the naturalist.

Most of her current work is environmental, not simply placing installations in an environment but changing the place itself. For example in her consultancy work for a transport company at Cradley Heath in Birmingham, she has helped to redesign the area between a bus station and a railway station.

Manheim has also been involved in performance art, sometimes in collaboration with others or on her own. The theme of remainders, leftovers and the discarded recurs throughout her work:

> A few years ago I made two sculptures for an exhibition called *Salvage* at the Festival Hall. One of the works was a cage structure which was upright and held two thousand folded newspapers. We could never have transported it full, it would have been too heavy. I made the cage and had it moved to the Festival Hall and there I was folding and pasting these newspapers which took two days and it almost became a little performance and that's when I discovered that I quite liked it. It was wonderful. Some people obviously ignored it because they think 'Ooh, that's a bit odd and I feel a bit wary', but other people come up to you and just talk to you or watch you. Sometimes I had very interesting and pertinent little conversations.

Simon Fraser became interested in jewellery as a small boy. He made jewellery for his aunts and cousins, particularly jewellery to wear for weddings. After his first degree at Sheffield Poytechnic he went into making production jewellery, creating large numbers of pieces in nylon. He was successful at this but felt unfulfilled and so started developing his jewellery as a vehicle for ideas and emotions. This shift was helped by an invitation from Brian Beaumont Nesbit asking Fraser to put work in a show on the theme of 'Love' for

Simon Fraser
Alchemy with a Piano, 1993
Piano components

Emma Paolozzi
Keyring amulets for the Freud Museum, London, 1996
Silver

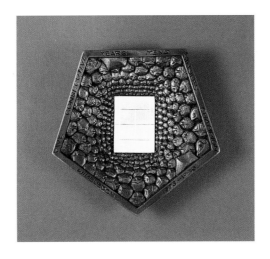

Fred Rich
Bjorn Borg medal, 1981 (obverse)
Bronze
Cast by the Royal Mint

Fred Rich
Bjorn Borg medal, 1981 (reverse)
Bronze
Cast by the Royal Mint

Fred Rich
Schools Curriculum Award Medal, 1984 (obverse)
Oxidised silver and parcel gilt
Cast by Hector Miller

Fred Rich
Schools Curriculum Award Medal, 1984 (reverse)
Oxidised silver and parcel gilt
Cast by Hector Miller

which he made jewellery based on the reproduction of primitive life forms such as protozoa. This also allowed Fraser to use a variety of materials for his work, *eg* dog biscuits in his late 1980s work *My Dog's a Vegetarian, Why isn't Yours?* His work cannot be called conceptual, it is less concerned with ideas about jewellery but more with a redefinition of why jewellery is made and worn. This does not imply a break with the past so much as a rediscovery of the potent individual and social meanings of jewellery.

This can be ritualistic, perhaps almost shamanistic as in his 1993 performance piece *Alchemy with a Piano*. Fraser transformed the space in the ICA in London by building steep seating on either side of the auditorium. This allowed the performance to take place on different physical levels. The products of the performance were pieces of jewellery, particularly crowns, made as the piano was taken apart. Most of the work was then auctioned for the London Lighthouse charity.

Caroline Broadhead, Susanna Heron and Julia Manheim have moved from the small scale of jewellery to create larger pieces of work and to engage with art and the environment. Other jewellers have developed their work into the realms of art but only on a smaller scale, one more closely related to that of jewellery. As Peter Dormer wrote in 1995: 'Making small things with large meanings confers a different image of "the artist" from the one most current in late twentieth-century art – that of the artist as hero or heroine working on a large scale.'[12]

Some have chosen to work in this smaller scale but have also moved away from traditional jewellery into creating objects with meaning that are not neccessarily worn.

Emma Paolozzi has created a series of amulet-like pieces of jewellery based on the ancient, sacred objects which Sigmund Freud collected and placed around his North London consulting room. He used these to symbolise psychological states and some of the internal myths that characterise 'the talking cure'. It has been suggested that jewellery might re-develop the role of 'amulet', as more than decoration or a good luck charm. If this is the case the area of dispute between art and jewellery can be better explored.

Others are working in the field of medals, which are small bas-relief works that are cast. The making of medals might seem like a small and specialist field of jewellery-related art. It is not a format for the grand gesture but within the small compass of the bas-relief medal, large themes can be commemorated and personal meanings explored. In an article in *The Medal* Mary Leavitt Brown writes of the difficulty of deciding on a common set of terms for medal-making: 'The only real parameters that were established were that a medal should be able to be held in the hand ... that the two sides should bear a relationship to each other; that the edges should be engaged to lead the hand and eye into discovering that relationship.'[13]

Medals tend to be small, hand-sized in scale or designed to be pinned onto garments, but they have resonant meanings. They are a clear link with antiquity from the Roman tradition of striking coins and medals to celebrate heroes and victors. It is perhaps this association with the past that causes as much disquiet with the viewer of the medal as the small size and reproducibility. Before the age of mechanical reproduction, medals and circles did reproduce images of the great, the good and the mythic. Mark Jones writes: 'Medals are multiples and multiples create unease in a public used to the idea of the work of art as the unique expression of the artist's feeling'.[14]

Fred Rich is most well known for his extraordinary enamels but he has also made notable contributions to the art of the medal.

In 1981 he entered the RSA Design Bursary medal section for the commemoration of a sporting event. For this he designed and modelled a medal celebrating Bjorn Borg's achievements in tennis. The medal was then cast by the Royal Mint. The obverse shows Bjorn Borg within a pentagram symbolising his five successive Wimbledon victories from 1976 to 1981. The reverse shows rows of centre court seats and umbrellas so that the medal is as much a humorous testimony to the regular wet weather during the tournament fortnight as a celebration of tennis. Rich finds that working on medals allows him to indulge his playfulness: 'That's what I love about medals, you've got the two sides and you can afford to be very serious on one side and you can afford to take the mickey out of it on the other side.'

Rich also created a medal for the School Curriculum Award Scheme in 1984. We look down onto a scene of happy children, playing on the obverse. It depicts children picking up fruits from the tree of knowledge. Their bodies wrap around the edge of the medal to the reverse where one finds an amusing classroom. This medal encapsulates the Scheme's sentiment of giving an award to a school whose curriculum involved the local community.

Jane McAdam Freud was a student at Central between 1978 and 1981. She chose to take a course in jewellery design because she believed that a lot of fine artists did jewellery as a bonus and she wanted additional skills as an artist.

McAdam Freud made her first medal as an entry to the RCA bursary competition in 1981. The medal she made was of Pablo Picasso, in bronze. A portrait head takes up one side of the asymmetrical medal whilst on the reverse is a head taken from the Picasso painting *Le Rêve*. The dual nature, the two sides of a medal and working in bas-relief gave her the direction that she needed in her work:

> It taught me that I didn't want to make jewellery and it gave me all the skills I needed to make objects and sculpture – modelling and carving. It allowed me to make an informed choice about what I wanted to do. Medals were a bridge between jewellery and sculpture. I feel a compulsion to say something through the work and jewellery didn't allow me to do that. It was also too decorative. The medal was such a strong vehicle – I'd never have found it if I hadn't been to Central.

The British Museum bought the medal and commissioned its reproduction for the British Art Medal Society which was sold to help fund a scholarship to the Scuola dell'Arte della Medaglia (School of the Art of the Medal) in Rome. The scholarship aimed to 'train people in the art of low-relief carving because the sculpture schools were turning people out with installation skills or conceptual skills but not actual carving and modelling skills. The figure was "out" at that time and it was all that post-modern stuff so I applied and got it for three years. It was fantastic. I went to the Accademia di Bella Arte where I did a sculpture course as well, so I was able to loosen up a bit. It was bliss, heaven.'

On her return to Britain, McAdam Freud worked for the Royal Mint as an 'engraver'. This was a misnomer since they no longer do hand-engraving and most of her work was designing and modelling. She also worked on a one-year medal project at the RCA where she found that medals as sculpture were treated as commemorative and it was quite difficult to convince people at the RCA that collecting old Coke cans was relevant.

Now McAdam Freud works in a variety of scales. She makes large stone carvings and spends a week a month working on coins, and still makes medals. In her booklet *Sculpture: On the Edge* she describes her interest in the way that medal-like objects are struck from the detritus of the streets or found in archaeological remains. 'Our streets abound with objects that have undergone processes of deformation which emulate the process of striking a medal. These objects have been lost or discarded and may be crushed by the weight of passing traffic. Their flattened form reverses the process employed in the modelling of low-relief for cast medals. An unintentional or elemental medal is thus created, its transient and uncontrived nature presenting a freshness of random form.'[15]

1 Clare Phillips, *Jewelry from Antiquity to Present*, Thames and Hudson, 1996, p.195

2 Rosalind Krauss, 'Sculpture in the expanded field', in Foster *et al.*, *Postmodern Culture*, Pluto Press, 1985

3 Peter Dormer, in Helen Drutt English, *Jewelry of Our Time: Art, Ornament and Obsession*, Thames and Hudson, 1995, p.68

4 Ralph Turner, *Jewelry in Europe and America: New Times, New Thinking*, Thames and Hudson, 1996, p.17

5 *Ibid.* p.22

6 Deborah Norton, 'Caroline Broadhead: jewellery and beyond', *Metalsmith*, vol.14, no.1, Winter 1991, p.42

7 Caroline Broadhead, quoted in John Houston, *Caroline Broadhead: Jewellery in Studio*, Bellew Publishing, 1990, p.50

8 Caroline Broadhead, *New Tradition: The Evolution of Jewellery 1965–1985*, British Crafts Centre, 1985, p.48

9 David Ward, *The Jewellery Project*, Crafts Council, 1983, p.7

10 Rose Slivka, 'New departures in jewellery', *Crafts*, no.64, September/October 1983, p.45

11 Barbara Cartlidge, quoted in James B. Evans, 'Silver and Electrum', *Metalsmith*, vol.17, no.2, Spring 1997, p.27

12 Peter Dormer, *op.cit.* p.84

13 Mary Leavitt Brown, 'Medal making at Central Saint Martins', *The Medal*, no.25, Autumn 1994, p.98

14 Mark Jones, *Contemporary British Medals*, British Museum Publications, 1986, p.16

15 Jane McAdam Freud, *Sculpture: On the Edge*, Yorkshire Museum, 1996

Jane McAdam Freud
Picasso medal, 1981
(obverse)
Bronze
Cast by Lunts

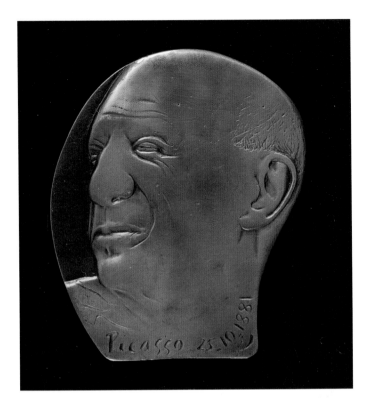

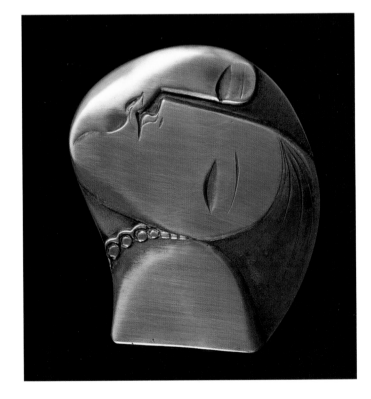

Jane McAdam Freud
Picasso medal, 1981
(reverse)
Bronze
Cast by Lunts

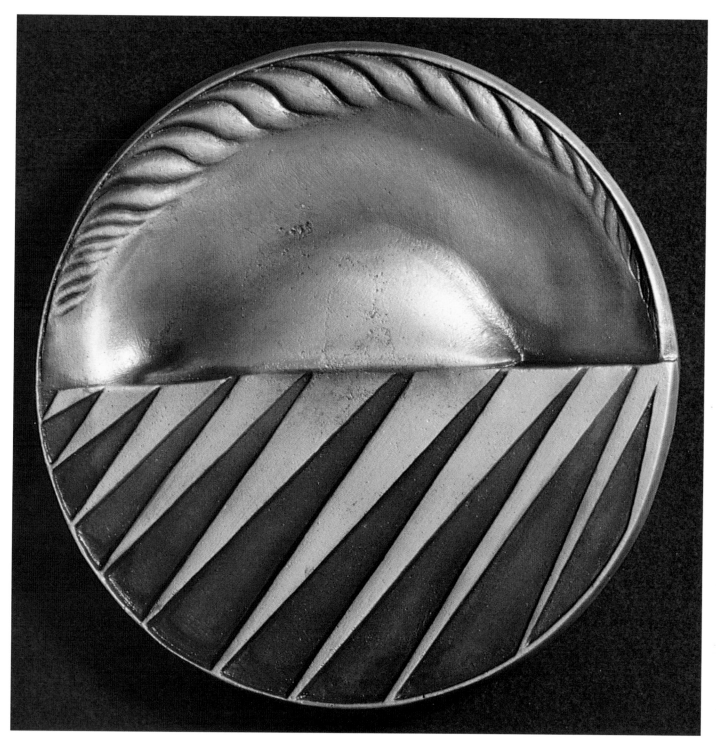

Jane McAdam Freud
Forked eye, 1992
Bronze

Jewellery & Fashion

Reema Pachachi
Necklace, 1991
Sterling silver and sard agate

Metals and jewels enhance the aura or radiance in which adornment shrouds the body. Simmel literally sees the body as shinier, more mirror-like when fashionable accessories are metallic.[1]

Fashion and jewellery go hand in hand. Jewellery is often the punctum, the half-registered detail that brings fashion alive.[2] It is hard to imagine the clothes of Elsa Schiaparelli without the extravagant surrealist jewels designed by Jean Schlumberger, or Chanel's modernist couture without the exuberant tumble of jewellery from the Duc de Verdura.

Fashion jewellery in the proper sense of the term are pieces made with attention to the demands of the fashion world without any loss of quality in design or manufacture. The jewellers interviewed are interested in fashion and have pursued a career based wholly or in part on that interest. Fashion is the most eclectic of jewellery design areas and the jewellers interviewed illustrate three typical career paths relating to fashion: those who collaborate with fashion designers and produce jewels specifically to complement the clothes, as Mick Milligan did in his designs for Zandra Rhodes or Peter Page's extraordinary 18-carat gold and diamond mask made for Ossie Clark's 1972 catwalk show; those who work independently of any specific fashion designer but whose work is closely allied to the industry, such as Wright and Teague; and others such as Dinny Hall, Nuala Jamison and Emma Paolozzi who have worked in both ways.

Gerda Flöckinger has been obsessed by fashion throughout her career as a jeweller. Fashion, she says, has been crucial in her life: 'Fashion and image or image and fashion. I find the development of clothing and the attitudes that human beings have to what they put on themselves fascinating. There is cultural snobbery about fashion as part of popular culture.'

After her time as a jewellery student at Central, Flöckinger went to work briefly for Bialkevic-Sphinx Femina, the fashion jewellers. Her ambition was to make modern jewellery and she welcomed the interest shown in her work by Mary Quant and Alexander Plunkett-Greene.

> Mary and Alexander came into Central in 1954 and Mary still looked very art studenty. They said they were going to start a boutique and that they wanted new jewellery, modern jewellery, nothing boring. They never sold very much of my work but it was a wonderful shop, most of the English at the time were so frumpy and backward-looking. They also commissioned work for themselves from me, I made their wedding rings which were huge, thick, wide gold rings.

The uneasy, yet potentially fruitful relationship between jewellery and fashion has still not become any easier since the mid-1950s. Nuala Jamison was exasperated with what she saw as an overtly traditional approach to materials when she was a student. She wanted to experiment with plastics but felt that the majority of the staff at Central were dismissive of new materials and fashion jewellery. One exception, Jamison recalls, was Gilian Packard who was familiar with the work of some of the experimental jewellers in the US and mainland Europe. She also welcomed the technical help she received from one of the technicians, Ted Leech, and Jamison valued the workshop situation in which students were taught.

Jamison currently teaches jewellery and three-dimensional design in higher and adult education in London and laments the dearth of equipment available to today's students compared to the generous provision of the late 1960s and early 1970s. Perhaps surprisingly, given her interest in fashion and in new materials, she received a training grant from the Worshipful Company of Goldsmiths to work with the mass-market jewellery manufacturers Fred Mansell

Peter Page
Mask for Ossie Clarke, 1972
18-carat gold and diamonds

who produce inexpensive 9-carat gold jewellery for high-street jewellers and mail order catalogues. It is easy to dismiss this kind of jewellery, which can hardly be called precious either in terms of material, design or make, yet this is the jewellery that many people buy, give and treasure, and it has a particular significance. Jamison's approach to this work was evangelistic and she strove to bring a greater sense of design to the high-street jeweller. Despite her efforts, however, the experience was not a happy one:

> I went to work for them and tried to do a little bit of design but it was impossible. The managing director used to go to Italy and France, buy something and copy it. That was his idea of design. At the same time I wrote a book, a little booklet about the World Gold Council who sponsored me, and by doing this, it made me realise that I didn't want to work in that sort of industry.

With the exception of a few specialist ranges such as Dinny Hall's *DHC* range of silver and acrylic pieces for Ernest Jones and Selfridges, little has changed in the windows of Britain's high-street jewellers since the 1970s. The high street remains largely impervious to design ideas in jewellery. It is perhaps the conservatism of the consumer and therefore of the retailer that has prevented designer-jewellers who are interested in fashion from having a greater impact on the high street.

After a brief time in a workshop run by Gilian Packard, Jamison moved to Covent Garden, London, with two other former Central students, Caroline Broadhead and Julia Manheim, and stayed there for twelve years. Initially the three worked separately but soon Broadhead and Jamison began to collaborate on work in perspex, specifically for the fashion industry. Broadhead and Jamison put three days a week into their company, C and N Accessories, but also continued with solo projects. Jamison describes their collaboration:

> By about 1978 I had started designing buttons for Jean Muir. Caroline and I decided to go into business together to see if we could make a little money. We did the first samples by hand, got orders and then found someone to cut [the work out]. I have been working for Jean Muir Ltd since then.

Jean Muir was a patron of the crafts and was concerned to promote and collect the solo work of both jewellers as well as commissioning them to design accessories for her shows and collections. Apart from having the buttons cut commercially they did all the work themselves. The work might have looked mass-produced but it was, in fact, batch-produced on a large scale. This meant that the buttons were made with the characteristic care and attention that one would expect from craft-production. Details and colour were altered to please each designer, and Caroline Broadhead recalls the amount of dedication it took to achieve this flexibility.

> I suppose the most we did was probably five to ten thousand buttons of each lot. People looked at the buttons and said 'Oh! you should be doing jewellery'. So we were brought into jewellery because that's what people wanted. We did quite a lot of fashion jewellery and then we realised that we were putting quite a bit of effort into making jewellery for the catwalk and even if it looked great, the jewellery buyers weren't at the shows. It may have impressed a lot of people, it may have made the clothes look great, but actually we weren't making any money out of it.

The financial rewards may not have been great but Nuala Jamison remembers this as a fertile period for collaborations between jewellers and fashion designers.

> At that time [the late 1970s and early 1980s] there were quite a lot of fashion designers in London who were doing quite well. We did buttons, dyed then polished up. Technically we were quite good … we should have had more of it done out [in a factory] but you could

never get anyone to finish them properly. They always
used to be hand polished .... Our buttons were very
expensive, they were only for designers and they were
difficult to make.

Broadhead recollects the button-making years:

We wanted something that we could make in the
workshop, possibly in production, and we thought
buttons would be a good idea because they're small ...
using the same materials that Nuala was using [chiefly
perspex] so she had a lot of knowledge about it. It just
seemed like an interesting thing. It was allied to
jewellery and yet it was part of something else. We did
the first collection for Jean Muir in 1978 and we
worked for her right up until she died, seventeen years
later. Sometimes we did five collections a year.

Caroline Broadhead also made jewellery for fashion on
her own, including a collection in cotton and other
textiles for Bruce Oldfield in 1974. This developed
from her earlier experience of colouring ivory.

I started carving ivory and giving it a sense of illusion
so that it looked as if it were flowing or it could be
knotted, or it looked like it could be a flexible material
and then I started introducing colour for ivory. I was
just doing this with a scalpel and introducing coloured
inks (I found out later it was called scrimshaw). Then I
decided to carry on with the colour and drop the ivory
so I started doing some things with cotton. These were
intended to be sold through boutiques and dress shops,
to be a fashion thing rather than exhibited.

Her remarks reflect a feeling that she and many other
jewellers had in the 1970s and 1980s, a feeling that
jewellery should not be based on precious materials
but should be made from appropriate and sympathetic
materials, sometimes with specific symbolic meanings.
An example of this approach is Broadhead's bracelets
from c.1980 made from the materials of domestic
brushes, wood and nylon bristle which were designed

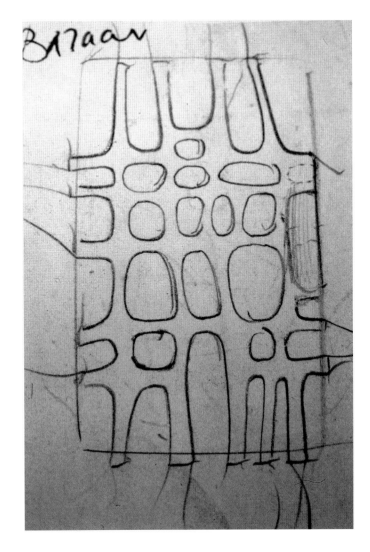

Gerda Flöckinger
Pendant for Mary Quant, 1955
Drawing

Gerda Flöckinger
Cufflinks, 1994
18-carat gold, pearls, garnet and enamel

Reema Pachachi

I used to do a great deal of work for fashion designers. Now, although I am still interested in fashion and I use the fashion cycle of seasons to pace my work, I am more interested in developing my jewellery in a way that is sympathetic to fashion but is independent of the work of fashion designers.

I love fashion and making jewellery for fashion. I also enjoy working in different materials using different methods; I used to make jewellery in PVC and in metal. Although I now make precious jewellery, I'm still aware of the fashion system and that helps to keep my work fresh.

Reema Pachachi
Necklace, 1991-2
Silver mesh chain, plaited with silver pendant shapes

partly as a commentary on female domestic servitude.

In 1992, C and N Accessories was dissolved and Nuala Jamison and Caroline Broadhead no longer work together. Broadhead has moved from jewellery to fine art but Jamison continues to work in fashion jewellery and over the years has worked for Vivienne Westwood, Jasper Conran and Jeff Banks as well as for Jean Muir.

Jamison found the ethos of making jewellery for fashion shows and collections different from working as a traditional jeweller. She finds the fashion world more frenetic and less well-planned. While this can be a strain it is compensated for in part by the sense of teamwork that exists within the fashion business, a sense of working together for a common aim usually fostered by the tight deadlines.

She is pessimistic about the future of jewellery, and feels that 'the industry in this country is going downmarket. If you go to Italy they want the best whereas in England they want the cheapest. Also, the difficulty now is that there are too many jewellers ... everybody thinks they can make jewellery.'

Jamison has built a reputation through twenty years of work and, despite her pessimism, is not disheartened. She still makes jewellery, retaining the simplicity and fine finish for which her work has always been noted. The necklace illustrated looks simple, with graduated turquoise and white pebbles of perspex, but each component is carefully balanced and the piece sits perfectly on the wearer. She describes her current solo work, which is not produced for fashion designers, in these terms:

> It's contemporary jewellery but it's not fashion. It's connected to fashion – it's how it's sold not what it is. All jewellery is designed for the body, it's made to wear. As a jeweller, I like making things for people to wear. I'm not interested in so-called art that's not one thing or another because you fall between two stools. People think jewellery is precious if it's made of precious materials. Jewellery has to have the feeling but not necessarily a precious material. It's got to have 'oooh!'.

Dinny Hall was a student at Central from 1978 until 1981. She feels that the course's concentration on design and techniques gave her 'the ability to see my ideas through from a technical point of view. Three years of being able to design things is great anyway: I didn't need to go to the RCA because I knew where I was going! I learnt my craft [at Central] and that was very important to me. I always knew that I wasn't going to go the straightforward route.'

Hall recalls that the first sign of her interest in jewellery was when as a child she swapped her Sindy doll for her mother's engagement ring. After graduating from Central she worked for a year with Martin Baker, who had a workshop in Lexington Street, London, and started selling her own work to Liberty and Harvey Nichols. At the same time she began working with fashion designers she had known during her student days:

> I started doing fashion shows for people like Rifat Ozbek, Bruce Oldfield, Isaac Mizrahi. I wouldn't say this was nepotism. When I was partying while I was at college those were the people I was partying with. [It was] a particularly creative period of time and [my friends] were at Saint Martins or the LSE or London College of Printing at the same time. You then get carried along on a media wave.

In the 1980s she found a receptive audience for her work in North America and for a while was more successful there than in Britain because 'they were complete consumerists, they were spending like hell and it all came plummeting down with the recession'.

Hall continued to design jewellery for fashion until the early 1990s. In 1989 she was voted 'British Accessory Designer of the Year' by the British Fashion Council. Her work for Rifat Ozbek's *New Age* collection in 1990 was pale, monochrome and cool, using clear perspex, sandblasted resin and sterling silver to complement his silver and white clothes. She described her aim in making jewellery as the creation of jewellery which is right for the time but which will never feel dated.

Hall tackled the British market by expanding her business and ensuring that she had more control over the production and retail of her work. She had already launched her wholesale jewellery business in 1984 and she made ranges in silver and gold-plated silver for Debenhams while selling her own work in established specialist stores. In the diffusion collection, *Dinny Hall Mark*, she used the design ideas that she had developed for her main collection which were drops based on Islamic domes and curlicues inspired by leaf growth patterns.

When she left Central her work had been in resin and plastics. She gradually added silver to her jewellery until in 1990 she started to work in 18-carat gold. This shift, she says, was because gold had become more fashionable. Like Caroline Broadhead and Nuala Jamison she found it worthwhile, creatively and financially, to listen to the consumer.

Fashion jewellery is important for women because it allows them to express the Self, rather than the feminine position of the Other. Most jewellery is bought by someone other than the wearer, and usually by men for women. The exchange of a gift or token often has a political and economic basis as well as an emotional one. The be-jewelled woman is the bearer of the look, the visual symbol of male wealth and power, by taking on the role of the conspicuous consumer. This can sometimes mean that the jewellery never belongs to the woman – it is not hers to dispose of as she wishes. It can also be seen as part of social surveillance. This is particularly true of fine jewellery, far less so of fashion jewellery which is usually bought by women for their own use. The buying and wearing of fashionable clothes and fashion jewellery are sources of creativity for women and, in the case of jewellery, a creativity not enjoyed by men who rarely buy jewellery for themselves.

Roland Barthes argues in *The Fashion System* that the details of fashionable dress are as, or more, important than the overall look: 'As for the genera most widely susceptible of meaning, we see that they are essentially not principal pieces but rather parts of pieces (collars or pockets) or accessory elements (pleats, fasteners, ornaments); this explains the importance fashion gives to "detail" in the production of meaning.'[3]

The meaning of fashion and jewellery is not only discerned and interpreted by the viewer but by the wearer. The experience of wearing jewellery, the feel of the materials, the contrast between metal and flesh, the weight of the jewellery cannot be imagined by someone who has never worn it. The ubiquitous watch and, perhaps, cuff-links may give an inkling of the feeling but few men wear jewellery in the way that women wear it.

Jane Adam regrets that jewellery is rarely discussed as something to wear as an adornment. It is usually seen as an image, two-dimensional, seen from the front and for the pleasure of the viewer; the problem or pleasure of wearing jewellery is rarely commented upon. Adam describes her work as reflecting the *zeitgeist* rather than fashion but she dislikes the negative judgements that are sometimes made about fashion jewellery and about women designing for women. She thinks that the best designers of jewellery are those who also wear it, that is primarily women. The charge of subjectivity levelled against women as fashion designers, with the implication that masculine objectivity somehow equals creativity is implicit, if not explicit in jewellery.

Although sometimes imperceptible in fashion photograph features and only fleetingly glanced in runway shows, jewellery is nevertheless important to fashion on all levels. Sometimes what is appropriate for the catwalk is inappropriate for the photographic feature. Nicholas Coleridge quotes Bruce Oldfield complaining about fashion editors: 'If the fashion editor plays around with the dress too much and puts gold twigs in the girl's hair, then it doesn't stand a chance.'[4]

Whether it was said first by Flaubert or Mies van der Rohe, 'God is in the Details' and, as fashion changes, so do the details. Dinny Hall recollects the changes in scale and material demanded by her customers in the early 1990s:

Nuala Jamison
Necklace, 1996
Silver and perspex

Nuala Jamison
Necklace, 1993
Silver and perspex

Dinny Hall
DHC jewellery for Ernest Jones and
Selfridges, *c*.1993
Silver

Things got smaller, it wasn't really fashionable to wear great huge things any more. So I could make things in silver and gradually more and more people were requesting gold pieces.

Her gold jewellery now accounts for around fifty percent of her sales. The purchase of non-precious fashion jewellery can be the stepping-stone to the purchase of precious jewellery. This is reflected in the high street where Marks & Spencer now sell 18-carat gold jewellery to supplement their costume jewellery range. Tom McEwan, the precious jeweller, has noticed that the 'ladies who lunch' who make up the majority of the wearers of his work have started buying their own precious jewellery and no longer rely on gifts from men.

In 1992 Hall opened her own shop in Westbourne Grove, London, where she also has her workshop. It was a bold step in the depths of a recession. The move stemmed from a new perception of her role. In the 1980s she had felt driven and the attraction was '... being new and pioneering ideas, being the first to do something. I had a fire behind me, a creative energy. It's not that it's gone, it's just that you can't do that all your life.'

Hall has encouraged young jewellers by employing them in her workshop. Elizabeth Olver remembers:

I started working for Dinny and putting work together for her collection. I could see what fashion jewellery was and its possibilities as far as I was concerned. It was design-led and design ideas have always fascinated me. I started putting together collections from then on. That was a terrifying and yet brilliant experience because it taught me about production in one fell swoop. I sold internationally. I used to sell to Holt Renfrew and Bergdorf Goodman in New York, through working with Dinny I learnt not to aim low.

From Hall's point of view the technical expertise brought in by jewellers such as Olver and Giles Last was essential but expensive, particularly as her business grew. The expansion led to a reassessment of her production methods. She employed trained jewellers to make up work from prototypes exactly as she wanted. It was an expensive and inefficient way of working. Eventually she decided to have her repetitive castings made in Thailand. The stones are set and the work is finished in her workshop.

This is a recurring theme in contemporary British jewellery: it is cheaper to have work made in the Far East and finished in Britain. This partly reflects the emphasis of art and design education: in the West we train our jewellers to be designers and/or craftsmen with the emphasis on the individual's contribution and expertise. The demise of the British manufacturing sector has meant that Britain provides the ideas and images but can no longer provide expertise on a commercial scale.

In 1995 Hall opened a shop in Fulham, London and has plans for two more, possibly in Manchester and Dublin, but she says that she has no global ambitions. She is a jeweller who has always enjoyed designing and working in three dimensions and has been inspired by architecture. She says, wistfully: 'As I grow older, I sometimes think that I would have liked to have been an architect.'

At Central, Dinny Hall was taught by Mick Milligan, whom she credits with stimulating her interest in fashion jewellery. Milligan was a self-taught jeweller who set up a workshop in Paris when he was nineteen. He returned to England and started attending Central as a part-time student in the following year. He then went to the RCA as an independent student and it was there that he became closely involved with fashion. He was dismayed to find that few of his fellow students were interested in the possibilities of collaboration with fashion designers and recollects:

Nobody seemed to realise that there was a Fashion Department in the Royal College and that you could put jewellery on a fashion show. I know I was the first person who said 'Look, I'll jewel the show' which to me is amazing, absolutely bewildering. I wanted to be an ornamental jeweller. I wanted to follow that tradition of ornamental design and improve on that and I think that's wonderfully valid. Fashion as a vehicle is fine because its pace is very fast and it allows possibilities.

His interest in jewellery for runway shows altered his perceptions of what was needed in fashion jewellery and he started developing large-scale jewels.

> I realised that there was no point in sending tiny rings down the runway – you're not there. It's a question of statement for effect, which is what a lot of jewellery is about – statements for effect. So I developed a rapport with the designer and I looked at the fashion designs and I interpreted them.

Milligan began working with Zandra Rhodes in 1970 when they collaborated on her *Button Flower* collection of that year. Using Rhodes's fashion sketches as a starting point he designed lily head-dresses, earrings and neckpieces from silver and gold-plated nickel for her first show at the Roundhouse, London in 1972. Zandra Rhodes describes the jewellery:

> It opened with the girls in specially beaded masks and progressed to golden lily necklaces on tremblers by Mick Milligan rustling around their necks to even the slightest movement.[5]

Milligan describes his work for Rhodes:

> Zandra Rhodes … is a unique designer to work with for sure. I worked with her for about ten years. When we did collections, sometimes three a year, I would take her imagery each time and re-interpret it in three dimensions, that would be my contribution. I was still doing what I was known for, which was romantic, naturalistic forms of jewellery which I liked as well. I now see that as being right in the arts and crafts inheritance.

In 1976 he worked on *The Cactus Cowboy Collection* creating gold cactus and arrow earrings, bracelets, pins and lariat rings for the runway show. His lightning brooches and arrow pins were frequently and blatantly copied. Milligan worked in many different materials, including aluminium foil for his bow chokers, 1974, and diamante for his ironic text necklace *Diamonds are a Girl's Best Friend* for Zandra Rhodes's own wear in 1972. The humour and experimentation of this work satisfied him in the 1960s and 1970s when he sold his work through Tommy Roberts's shop Mr Freedom in London. His work had the subversive quality of Pop art which, translated into jewellery, also challenged 'the pecuniary canons of taste': his were the first Mickey Mouse brooches in diamante! He described the 1970s as a very liberating period in terms of experimentation and a time when so many new things were happening.

In 1978 and 1979 Milligan took his expertise and eclectic approach to Central as a Visiting Tutor. He wanted his experience in fashion to be a warning to his students. Allthough he valued his work in the fashion world he found it difficult to make fashionable jewellery, particularly fashionable precious jewellery, without the aegis of a designer. He echoes Nuala Jamison's disquiet about the status of designer jewellery in Britain:

> It's not as if one didn't try to take it into the next stage. It's almost like an English in-built failing, you'll come up with these things that look wonderful and you cannot get them into further manufacturing … you went around jewellery companies and all they wanted to do was to make hedgehogs with diamond eyes or rip off your idea. There's a whole list of people who came through Central. They would get involved in a look that was low production, fashionable – some of them I taught. But I would say to them 'what you've got to do now is go to Italy … if you work there maybe you may go somewhere but otherwise you're in a pretty narrow band'. When you think of the thousands and thousands of jewellery students who come through no wonder half of them end up in a tiny room making a tiny little thing

Dinny Hall
Earring, *c.*1994
Silver

Dinny Hall
Rings, 1996
18-carat gold and gemstones

and being subsidised by something else.

A successful jeweller may be fashionable but he has got to be involved in relating money and jewellery together. Now you don't have to have money to make wonderful pieces of jewellery, that's self-evident, but at the same time you do have to find clients for it – otherwise what's the point? I like making jewels for people and seeing them being worn.

When one looks though *Aurum*, the trade magazine produced by the World Gold Council, the pages are full of fairly traditional designs from Italy, but very few from any other country. The annual jewellery trade exhibition, *VicenzaOro*, is partly sponsored by the Italian government. This domination of the trade side of jewellery makes it difficult, as Nuala Jamison pointed out, for British designer-jewellers to develop in that area. It is because Italian jewellery buyers are seen by the trade as having superior taste that mainly Italian designs are adapted for the high street. Yet these translations of jewellery tend to be clumsy and often in low-carat gold reinforcing the notion of symbolic exchange but not the skill of the jeweller.

Milligan is still a jeweller but works only to commission nowadays. He works on his own or with Tom Scott, with whom he shares a workshop in London. His interest in the use of materials and the development of skill and craftsmanship as well as design is as evident now as it was when he started his career.

I now have nothing to do with fashion jewellery. What had happened was that people had forgotten that I made precious jewellery. [But] the whole thing felt right at the time. It was a lovely time, you were surrounded by swirls of colour and glamour and girls but no money. I now find it very challenging just to make precious jewellery statements .... I'm not interested in making new decorative art statements like a lot of other jewellers are. I'm a very traditional person and I do see my lineage as being from Oxfordshire Arts and Crafts and I am still involved in natural figurative design.

Gary Wright and Sheila Teague met at Central when they were students in the early 1970s. Teague did a foundation course at Plymouth College of Art and spent a year on the jewellery course at Birmingham Polytechnic before joining the Central course. Wright studied fashion design at Jacob Kramer College in Leeds and worked as a jeweller for two years before going to Central. He says: 'I have always related the two – fashion and jewellery – together .... I always thought of them as one and the same thing – it is all about the body, after all.'

At Central, Wright's work was fashion-orientated but it was not superficially pleasing. He describes it in these terms:

Literally everything I made then [was] figurative or had some meaning, not exactly deep psychological meaning. Some were tongue in cheek ... like the spent match brooches: a pink bowl of plastic cherries that I remember Ralph Turner bought for the Crafts Council Collection. Only last year it was in an exhibition they had there ... flies and maggots that were in one large necklace. Then I started doing maggot earrings and fly earrings and little-man earrings.

Looking back, he is critical of this early work:

You just kind of do certain things that you look at when you're at college, because there are no inhibitions or anything ... after a few years you realise that you should have done it another way and a bit stronger.

After leaving Central he worked at 401$\frac{1}{2}$ Workshops in South London making pieces in silver. At this stage he and Teague worked seperately although they toured Australia and South-East Asia together in 1977 and then shared a Clerkenwell workshop. In 1980 they started designing and producing joint collections under the name 'Wright and Teague'. Their ideas on jewellery coincided and they found that they both worked best in metal, initially brass or phosphur bronze and then in sterling silver or gold-plated silver.

Tom McEwan
Necklace, 1991
18-carat gold, amethysts, brilliants and enamel

Tom McEwan
Rings, 1996
Gold, silver and
gemstones

Mick Milligan
Flower necklace and matching ring, 1983
Red and yellow 18-carat gold, diamonds mother of pearl and enamel

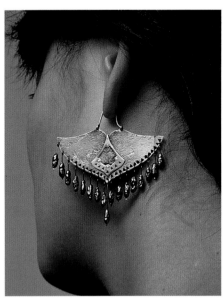

Elizabeth Olver
Earring, 1994
Silver

Their target market was fashionable women and they were aware of the importance of effective marketing. With international ambitions Wright realised that they had to be pro-active:

> We'd sell in high-class department stores and boutiques and also, apart from the jewellery, we had bags, scarves, gloves, shoes – a total accessory look. We designed them and had them made in factories. We used to do exhibitions and we were really geared up towards the fashion industry, so we'd show in Paris when it was Paris fashion week. By doing the fashion shows or trade shows in Paris, international buyers who were over there to buy clothing could come and see us. We've got about fifty outlets around the world.

From 1992 until 1996 Wright and Teague worked only in sterling silver, which has the benefits of ductility and responsiveness and is relatively inexpensive. Their silver designs, such as the simple bangles from 1985 which appeared in fashion photographs worn twenty-two deep, have always been their best sellers. They limited their dependence on the fashion cycle by gradually adding designs to their existing range rather than by producing new collections. Teague speaks of their collections:

> We used to design new collections twice a year – Spring and Autumn – but now we realise that there is more longevity in what we do and we can just add and subtract to a collection. A lot of the customers that we have may have ten or twenty pieces of our jewellery and they collect it. They also find that something they bought ten or fifteen years ago is still fairly current.

Sheila Teague sees flexibility as central to their success. She believes that jewellery skills have to be made to adapt to so many different areas. They have designed and made jewellery for film, theatre and television – a lucrative, although easily overlooked, area of the jeweller's craft.

Despite their success Wright and Teague maintain a practical approach to their jewellery and their methods of working have changed little since they were students. They keep examples of all their work, allowing them to assess their own development as designers and to re-create a piece if they wish. Sheila Teague says:

> We are very hands-on in what we do and I like making things anyway. That's what gives our work an edge. Gary makes all the patterns so we've got control over everything we do, we do lots and lots of drawings. There is that one-off impetus in the first place and then the idea is to make every other piece look as near [the original] as we can. We really spend hours and hours considering every last detail.
>
> We still think of ourselves as craftsmen rather than anything else ... the business side is the hideous, horrible side; the making and the designing is the plus. The other bit goes with the territory. We are design led rather than market led – we have that luxury. We have never had to make anything that we didn't like.

The consumer is also important to them. Wright and Teague jewellery is bought to be worn, not for its investment value. However, it does last and keeps its value as jewellery and as an adornment.

> People do keep our things for a long time. People bring back earrings they've had for ten years, distraught because the ear wire's come loose, but you couldn't really do that with clothing and I think that's what's really nice about jewellery – it's that longevity and that tradition. That's the terrifying thing: these people's daughters want to buy things now.

They are gradually changing the nature of their work and the market for it. In 1996 they launched a collection in 18-carat gold and diamonds. Teague sees this work as complementing the silver jewellery, saying it 'will add percentage to the silver work. It's only worth putting it in a shop that really knows about jewellery.'

This is a recurrent theme. Not only does the jewellery have to be 'good' in terms of design and make – it also has to be marketed correctly, and this marketing needs to be kept under review. Shops such as Harvey Nichols and Liberty together with galleries and specialist jewellery shops like Jess James provide a service to the consumer and to the jeweller.

The retailer has tremendous power. In his book *The Fashion Conspiracy*, Nicholas Coleridge sees a triangular structure of power in fashion comprising the designer, the buyer and the magazine fashion editor, the last of whom being the most powerful because he or she decides whose work will be promoted, unless the designer is part of a small élite who can dictate the image of their work. In the jewellery trade the buyer or gallery owner holds the power, not least because most jewellery is on sale or return, especially if the jeweller is relatively unknown. Some jewellers do resent this if they feel that the retail mark-up is excessive, but the difficulty lies with the jeweller being unable to sell his or her own work easily.

David Poston addresses this problem in his essay in the *What is Jewellery?* exhibition catalogue for the Crafts Council, London in 1995. 'Just as the crafts world tends to look mainly at the object and its maker than at its user, so it also largely ignores the retailers who market the work. However, if there is a translation between the states of being a product and a possession it is the retailer who makes it possible through a connection of the two different intimacies, making and owning/wearing.'[6]

Not only is the shop or gallery a source of revenue or a contact point between buyer and maker, it is also often a source of inspiration and information for the jeweller. Nuala Jamison cites the Electrum Gallery, founded by Barbara Cartlidge in 1971, as a major source of new ideas. Younger jewellers find the gallery just as important. Sally Anne Lowe, who left Central in 1993, says of Electrum:

Even though it's only one person's view of contemporary jewellery, you see things from all over the world. The Crafts Council is very British and I'm quite influenced by Japanese jewellery.

Sally Anne Lowe is also practically helped by the Electrum Gallery by working there part-time, as does another ex-student, Anna Opher, who has also worked in the Jewellery Department at Liberty and Dower and Hall in Knightsbridge. Opher feels that by selling other people's work, she has learned how to sell her own.

Jess Canty, who owns Jess James, the contemporary fashion jewellery shop in Newburgh Street, London, provided similar help to Harriet Russell who left Central in 1989. Oonagh Hefford who runs two jewellery shops called Penelope Red with her business partner Jansei Sullivan, reiterates the importance of education in jewellery:

I've come across jewellers who haven't been through the art school system and they've really struggled and don't have the confidence. We only employ jewellers. Everybody we take on works in the shop, at the bench and does some paper work. It's good for them because they learn all the ropes.

You would think that because we are on a high-street location, that people will only be interested in diamond engagement rings, but a surprising number will come in and buy interesting jewellery. These are people who wouldn't dream of going to a gallery but then we are selling it as jewellery and we are not pretending that it is art or anything else. There are so few jewellery shops left where someone can come in and talk to a designer and have something created for them. Most of our staff are designers who we take on mainly from Epsom and Medway. Leo de Vroomen gets the best and we get the pick of the rest.

After graduating, Sally Anne Lowe went to the RCA where for one of her major projects she designed large spun-metal handbags. She was inspired by the catwalk and she regarded fashion as a natural arena for her

Wright and **Teague**
Jewellery, 1996
Sterling silver

Wright and **Teague**
Rings and pendants, 1996
18-carat gold, enamel and gemstones

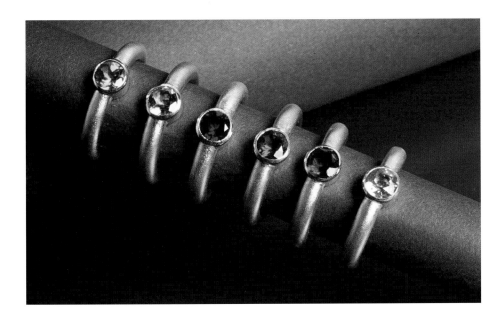

Anna Opher
Rings, 1997
Silver and gemstones

Sally Anne Lowe
Neckpiece, 1992
Silver

Sally Anne Lowe
Neckpiece, 1992 (close-up)
Silver

work. In 1996 she had a chance to work in collaboration with a fashion company called AD. Like Lowe, they had been helped by a loan and business advice from the Prince's Trust and together they put on a fashion show.

> AD were producing a catwalk show in London Fashion Week, but at separate premises which they hired, and they were doing the music and lighting, everything. They saw my work through a stylist who'd used my rings for a pop video because when I left college my bigger pieces got a bit of interest from fashion people. I got some gorgeous photographs out of it by a professional photographer with the models and wonderful clothes by AD. But there was no money in it.

This is reminiscent of the experiences of Nuala Jamison, Caroline Broadhead, Dinny Hall and Mick Milligan and this will hopefully mark the beginning of a new series of creative partnerships between jewellery and fashion. Sally Anne Lowe is optimistic but is concentrating on designing and making jewellery for her own projects at the moment. On balance she does not think British fashion designers in the late 1990s appreciate jewellers:

> I feel that a lot of fashion designers plump for quite safe jewellery; even the quite innovative fashion designers are rather staid when it comes to jewellery.

And indeed, some jewellers question whether fashion designers understand jewellery at all. Jos Skeates and Ruaridh McIntyre set up a partnership after leaving Central in 1996. They have done some production work for Emma Paolozzi, and made buttons for Nicole Farhi but their ambition is to have a shop and a workshop along the lines of Jess James and to make fashion jewellery, not jewellery for fashion. In other words, they wish to set the fashion in jewellery and not respond to the demands of fashion designers. Jos Skeates feels that few fashion designers understand jewellery and yet they feel free to design it.

> We went to Liberty the other day to look at the fashion jewellery section where people like John Galliano and Jean Paul Gaultier have their lines of jewellery. They were just disgusting. I thought here is a man who does not understand jewellery on any level even as body adornment and it's very expensive. Of course if it's well-made and well-designed then people should pay and people don't mind paying if it's the bollocks.

Skeates and McIntyre would like to see some of the attitudes that consumers have to fashion develop with regard to jewellery:

> The pace of change in jewellery is very slow. If you could cross the boundary to the pace of fashion you'd be laughing. If people said 'Jos and Ruaridh have brought out a new range of jewellery so I can't wear last year's', that would be great.

Emma Paolozzi feels that fashion designers sometimes use her work as a focus of excitement within their designs. She designs jewellery for two London-based fashion designers, Paul Smith and Nicole Farhi. Nicole Farhi's image is elegant and classic and the clothes are suitable for all age groups. For Farhi, Paolozzi designs jewellery for women and men which tends to be understated to complement the clothes. The jewellery is not easy to make, however, and she has found the creative relationship challenging and considers in retrospect that this enforced simplicity has helped her to refine and develop her work. She made wedding rings for Farhi and her husband, the playwright David Hare.

Paolozzi first approached Paul Smith in 1990 with a small collection of jewellery and the company have increased their orders ever since.

Through her work for Smith she has been able to design fashion jewellery for men rather than for women and she has produced mainly cuff-links and rings. 'I like his philosophy, he calls it classics with a twist. He will do a really impeccable suit for a man and my cuff-links are completely off the wall but they go with the whole feeling of it. I often think "Crikey, I've really gone over the top" but they love it.' As she says, the Paul Smith image is one of stylish eccentricity combined with traditional British design values and this has proved to be popular worldwide. One of Paolozzi's most successful pieces came from that global symbol of consumerism, the barcode:

> I make a real point with Paul Smith of not looking at what other people do. Sometimes I will just see something in the street, I'm not looking for jewellery imagery. For instance, last year one of their big sellers was my barcode ring. I did a ring in silver which I oxidised so that it was black and white in lines with numbers on. I also did barcode cuff-links – it's an international language, the Japanese loved it and people in Hong Kong loved it.

Paolozzi likes the Paul Smith way of working: the buyer will buy samples from her and show them to other Paul Smith buyers and licensees from other countries and orders are generated for which she is paid separately. This takes away much of the insecurity of the sale or return system. Paul Smith's success has been due in no small part to the changes in men's attitudes to fashion and consumption in the 1980s and 1990s. As Jennifer Craik writes:

> Throughout the 1980s, media and popular culture have anticipated the emergence of the rejuvenated peacock, a man who is aware of his body, not just as a machine but as an object of sexual attraction enhanced by his choice of clothes and ways of wearing them. The New Man rhetoric has accompanied the intensified pro-duction of male fashions and cosmetics .... The New Man chose Romeo Gigli, The Gap, Agnès B, and Nicole Farhi with Paul Smith tropical boxer briefs as underpants.[7]

This implies that The New Man approaches fashion in a spirit of rather eclectic and expensive bricolage. Of course, for many men a wardrobe comprising the work of well-known designers is not financially possible but the purchase of a pair of distinctive cufflinks indicates the ability to participate in this new world of male adornment and consumption rather better than a pair of underpants. However the cufflinks can also be seen to reinforce conventional male office dress because they have to be worn with a shirt that has double-cuffs, the most traditional kind of shirt which is rarely, if ever, worn without a suit. Jewellery in this case is a little piece of sanctioned rebellion as much as a sign of a new breed of dandy.

John Mack writes in *Ethnic Jewellery* that: 'Jewellery, of course, is only one part of body decoration. To that extent it is at once a precise and yet limited point of departure.'[8] Perhaps this is nowhere as true as in jewellery for fashion.

Another area of body decoration and jewellery that might be placed under the aegis of fashion is piercing. People have had their ears pierced for thousands of years to make wearing earrings easier and in different cultures, other parts of the body are pierced. In North Western India the woman's left nostril is pierced allowing a complicated wedding decoration to loop around the ear, so that this mode of piercing indicates feminity. The 'Prince Albert' is a practice whereby the foreskin is pierced with a chain that is then looped around the leg. The name and the practice come from Queen Victoria's consort who wanted to ensure a smooth line under tight-fitting trousers.

The practice of body piercing as a sexual or a sub-cultural practice increased during the 1980s and became diluted in meaning and in visual interest when indulged in by large numbers of adolescents. However, there has always been a strong underground movement dedicated to the practice of body piercing and this shows no sign of abating.

Soon after leaving Central Saint Martins, Russell Lownsborough decided on the course that his work should take after a chance meeting with Teena, an established body piercer:

Jos Skeates
Adjustable rings, 1996
Silver, gold, rock crystal, titanium and plastic

Ruaridh McIntyre
Watch, 1996
Sterling silver, rubber and perspex

Jos Skeates
Headpiece, 1994
Polyvinyl chloride

Jos Skeates and **Ruaridh McIntyre**
Headpiece, 1997
Aluminium
Made for Ninz, London Fashion Week, 1997

Emma Paolozzi
Jewellery, 1996
Silver
Made for Paul Smith

Emma Paolozzi
Cufflinks, 1995
Silver
Made for the opening of Nicole Farhi's
Bond Street shop

She thought I was the right kind of person to make up the piercing jewellery she needed in gold. I thought 'who the hell is going to want holes puncturing different parts of their body?'. But I needed the money and she provided me with more and more work. I thought they were all nutcases until I got my first piercing and I did get quite a buzz out of it. I said 'stick it in my navel' and I looked down and saw this enormous needle sticking through my belly – I just burst out laughing.

Some of it is just fashion. Everyone knew when Naomi Campbell had her navel done that it was one of mine. And it is linked in other ways because the jewellery fits certain parts of the body, so it's got to be comfortable under clothes – it mustn't catch and each person is quite different. The piercing swells and then calms down and sometimes they have to come back and be refitted. There is also the question of the amount of weight you can put on a piercing. I don't do much of the insertion myself.

I like to do bespoke jewellery, one-off pieces. Teena's got a lot of good clients who are prepared to spend a lot of money on something different.

Cultural critics such as Alistair Bennett have reservations about the body altering or mutilation activities of the Modern Primitives.[9] He sees these activities in terms of a non-critical obsession with an image of the exotic Other; a kind of play-acting, dressing up rather as Lawrence of Arabia or Nancy Cunard did in their colonialist fantasies earlier this century. Others see it as a direct attempt to re-possess individual power over the body taking on Mary Douglas's theory of the two bodies as their blueprint. By taking possession of their own bodies and decorating them in a way that is personally meaningful they can truly express themselves. 'The two bodies are the self and society: sometimes they are so near as to be almost merged; sometimes they are far apart. The tension between them allows the elaboration of meaning.'[10]

It is interesting that comparatively few jewellers have developed their work into this area, bearing in mind the scope that it potentially gives them to develop new kinds of jewellery and new ways of ornamenting the body. Lownsborough is aware of the homogenising effect of fashion and its ability to strip meaning from apparently the most shocking and bizarre subcultural forms and that style is always a hybrid.

Some people are into piercing for more esoteric reasons but I'm just interested in what I can do with the jewellery. It's pretty unexplored at the moment, there aren't that many people buying bespoke piercing jewellery. I don't make stainless steel stuff – that's light engineering not jewellery – I like gold, I like silver, I like precious stones and I've always wanted to make precious things.

I'm trying to blend Rococo and Victorian Gothic with high-tech stuff, experimenting to stop myself going stagnant, design-wise. I always carry a sketch pad with me; even if I'm on the floor dead drunk at a party I'll draw something but I might not understand it the next day. Sometimes it'll take a year for a design to grow from several other designs. The details on science-fiction models are fantastic – I love that. All the sci-fi stuff I read years ago is filtering through and you will see its influence more and more. I find practically all the cyber-punk stuff like William Gibson inspirational, there are great ideas in it.

It's taken quite a long time for piercing to move from sub-culture to mainstream, it originated of course in the Sado-Masochism and fetish scenes, where it has most meaning – now its only a matter of time before the Weetabix men are doing it too!

For most of the people involved in this book, their interview was a 'work-in-progress', a verbal snapshot of their practice of jewellery and related disciplines. It would be a fascinating exercise to follow them up, say, in ten years time and discuss the changes in the fields featured in this book. Materials and the relationships between art, fashion, jewellery and the body are the areas in which, I predict, some of the most dramatic changes in design will happen. Scilla Speet is equally optimistic about the future of jewellery:

In the 1980s and early 1990s there was a great deal of confusion as well as creativity in jewellery making. This was due to a variety of causes: fluctuating markets, real or imagined rivalry between jewellers working in different ways, the limited number of outlets selling jewellery and perhaps a general feeling in society that anyone can make jewellery. Now, the materials debate has settled, and exciting work is being produced in many materials and the development of new alloys is wonderful for making jewellery. For example, the new silver alloy with which I have been working allows me to bridge the divide between textiles and metal.

Other innovations, such as the development of CAD/CAM [Computer Aided Design/Computer Aided Manufacture] systems opens a wide range of possibilities for design and production. However, these developments are not necessarily to the detriment of craft skills in jewellery – they will always be important because they are the basic vocabulary of making. Some jewellers have rediscovered the importance of symbolism and meaning in jewellery and this is reflected by the public interest in jewellery. This interest has been encouraged by the opening of new shops that show the work of new designers and artists.

This book has shown the passionate attachment of jewellers to the beauty and variety of craft- and designer-jewellery exemplified in the notion of 'Made to Wear'.

1   Joanne Finkelstein, *After a Fashion*, Melbourne University Press, 1996, p.38

2   Roland Barthes, *Camera Lucida*, Fontana, 1982, p.27 'for punctum is also: sting, speck, cut, a little hole – and also a cast of the dice'

3   Roland Barthes, *The Fashion System*, translated by Matthew Ward and Richard Howard, University of California Press, 1990, p.183

4   Nicholas Coleridge, *The Fashion Conspiracy*, Mandarin, 1989, p.254

5   Zandra Rhodes and Anne Knight, *The Art of Zandra Rhodes*, Jonathan Cape, 1984, p.107

6   David Poston, *What is Jewellery?*, exh. cat., Crafts Council, 1995

7   Jennifer Craik, *The Face of Fashion: Cultural Studies in Fashion*, Routledge, 1994, pp.199–200

8   John Mack, *Ethnic Jewellery*, British Museum Press, 1988, p.10

9   Alistair Bennett, 'The new primitives', in *Variant*, no.16, Winter/Spring 1994, pp.54

10 Mary Douglas, *Natural Symbols: Explorations in Cosmology*, Penguin, 1973, p.93

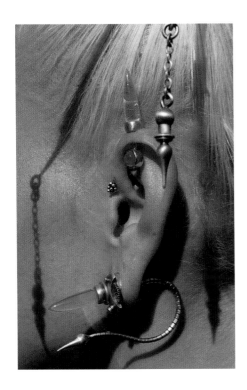

Russell Lownsborough
Ear jewellery, 1997
Gold, silver and gemstones

Russell Lownsborough
Piercing jewellery, 1997
Gold, silver and gemstones

Glossary

Jewellers' Biographies

Jewellers Interviewed

Glossary

Acrylic: A plastic material also known as perspex. It is a versatile and light material which can be moulded or cut or used in resin form and the finish can be clear, opaque, polished or ground to a matt finish and can be coloured.

Alloy: An homogeneous mixture of metals. An alloy usually has more useful characteristics than the individual metals *ie* it is more durable and fusible but often less malleable. *Electrum* is a naturally occurring alloy of gold and silver.

Brilliant-Cut: The method of cutting a diamond so that the light is not lost through the bottom of the stone, but is reflected up through the crown. This is achieved by cutting the facets around a horizontal girdle line which divides the stone into two unequal halves.

Cabochon: A stone cut without facets, so that it has a smooth, rounded surface, usually domed.

Carat ¹: A unit of weight used in jewellery making and goldsmithing used for all kinds of stones. Since 1914 the International Metric Carat has been 200mg or one-fifth of a gram.

Carat ²: The quality of a gold product or alloy. 24-carat gold is pure gold. 18-carat gold means that the gold content is 18/24ths and 9-carat gold is 9/24ths *ie* the gold content is a little over a third of the piece. The purity of gold can be expressed as a percentage, as it often is in Europe *eg* 18-carat gold is 75 percent.

Champlevé: This literally means 'raised field'. Designs are made into the metal and these areas are filled with coloured enamels which are then fired.

Cloisonné: In this technique, the areas to be enamelled on the piece are defined by thin wires or strips of metal. Sometimes these divisions are soldered into place or they can be held by an adhesive. The enamel is placed between the wires and the whole piece is fired.

Cubit Zirconium: A synthetic carbon stone which closely resembles the diamond in colour and refractive index and was first produced in the 1950s. It is slightly less hard than a diamond but generally can be used in the same way.

Electroforming: A technique developed in the nineteenth century to make copies of ancient jewellery. Either a mould is taken of the original piece and metal is deposited inside the mould by electrical current or the original object is used directly, thus giving a perfect reproduction.

Enamel: Glass material which is finely gound and has pigments and a flux added to it. The enamel is usually applied within the boundaries created by the *champlevé* or *cloisonné* techniques but can also be painted onto an object using an oil-based medium which evaporates during firing. Enamels can be opaque or transparent and a wide range of colours can be obtained. Texture can be created by engraving the metal under the enamel.

Hallmark: In Great Britain and some other European countries, the hallmark is used as a test of the worth of the metal and to identify when the piece was made. The British marks are: the Maker's or Sponsor's mark, the Assay Office mark identifies the place where it was hallmarked *eg*, the mark for London is a leopard's head, a Standard mark attests to the gold, silver or platinum content of the piece and the Date mark, is identified by a letter from a running series.

Pâté de verre: Flux and pigment are added to powdered glass to make up a glass paste. The paste is applied to the interior of a mould and and it is then fired. It makes very fragile and light pieces. The technique was developed in the nineteenth century.

Pliqué-à-jour: An enamelling technique in which the final effect is that of a stained-glass window. This is achieved by making a metal outline which is filled with transparent enamels. The enamel is either mixed with sufficient flux to ensure it does not run or a backing of copper foil is used to support the enamel which is then dissolved by acid.

Repoussé: The hammering and punching of a metal plate from the reverse to create a raised design at the front.

Rose-Cut: A stone cut with a flat back with two rows of facets rising to a point. The facets can be of different shapes and sizes.

Sterling Silver: An alloy used for jewellery containing 92.5 percent silver and 7.5 percent other metal, often copper.

Jewellers' Biographies

Jane Adam
Designer-jeweller, works in anodised aluminium
Studied: Manchester Polytechnic, 1978–81; Royal College of Art, 1982–5
Part-time tutor on the jewellery course at Central Saint Martins, 1994–7
Collections: Cooper-Hewitt Museum, New York; Crafts Council, London; Musée des Arts Décoratifs, Helsinki

Martin Baker
Designer-jeweller and silversmith, mainly works to commission. Some collaborations with Wartski
Studied: Central School of Art and Design, 1973–6; Royal College of Art, 1976–9
Part-time tutor on the jewellery course at Central School of Art and Design from 1980 onwards
Collections: The Worshipful Company of Goldsmiths, London

Caroline Broadhead
Currently involved in textile art objects
Studied: Leicester School of Art, 1968–9; Central School of Art and Design, 1969–72
Collections: Cleveland County Museum, Teesside; Crafts Council, London; Gemeentelijke van Reekummuseum, Apeldoorn, The Netherlands; National Museum of Modern Art, Kyoto; The Worshipful Company of Goldsmiths, London

Barbara Christie
Own practice as a jeweller since 1976, currently working on a new gold alloy
Studied: Sir John Cass College, 1972–6
Part-time tutor on the jewellery course at Central Saint Martins from 1991 onwards

Ros Conway
Own practice as a designer-jeweller and enameller since 1975, currently involved in making glass *objets d'art* using *pâté de verre*
Studied: Central School of Art and Design, 1970–3; Royal College of Art, 1973–5
Part-time tutor on the jewellery course at Central School of Art and Design in 1980
Collections: Crafts Council, London; Victoria & Albert Museum, London; The Worshipful Company of Goldsmiths, London

Roger Doyle
Own practice as a designer-jeweller, mainly making fine jewellery and clocks. Also works as a consultant to the industry. Freeman of The Worshipful Company of Goldsmiths
Studied: Jewellery apprenticeship at Cartier, and Central School of Arts and Crafts, 1965–6; Sir John Cass College, 1966–7
Part-time tutor on the jewellery course at Central School of Art and Design 1978–86
Collections: Victoria & Albert Museum, London; The Worshipful Company of Goldsmiths, London

Gerda Flöckinger CBE
Designer-jeweller, works in precious stones and metals
Studied: St Martins School of Art, 1945–50 and 1952–6
Collections: Schmuckmuseum, Pforzheim, Germany; Victoria & Albert Museum, London; The Worshipful Company of Goldsmiths, London

Georgina Follett
Currently Head of School of Design, Duncan of Jordanstone College, Dundee. Mainly involved in education management
Studied: Central School of Art and Design, 1968–71; Royal College of Art, 1971–4
External assessor on the jewellery course at Central Saint Martins from 1994 onwards
Collections: Crafts Council, London

Simon Fraser
Jeweller and performance artist
Studied: Sheffield City Polytechnic, 1982–5; Royal College of Art, 1991–3
Part-time tutor on the jewellery course at Central Saint Martins from 1996 onwards

Graham Fuller
Own established practice as a jeweller. Work with other jewellers includes collaborations with Roger Doyle and John Donald
Studied: West Sussex College of Art and Design 1961–3
Part-time tutor on the jewellery course at Central School of Art and Design from 1976 onwards

Patrick Furse
Long-established practice as a jeweller, enameller and painter. Previous work includes several large-scale enamelled murals with Stephan Knapp and Robin Banks
Studied: Chelsea College of Art, London, part-time during the 1940s and 1950s
Part-time tutor on the jewellery course at Central School of Art and Design, 1970–84

Dinny Hall
Own practice as a designer-jeweller with two shops in London selling ranges of fashion jewellery for fashion designers, collections and stores. Produces a fashion-jewellery collection each year
Studied: Central School of Art and Design, 1978–81
Won British Accessory Designer of the Year Award, 1989

Oonagh Hefford
Manager and buyer for UK and abroad purchasing fashion jewellery. Runs two shops with her partner Jansei Sullivan
Studied: Central School of Art and Design, 1982–5

Susanna Heron
Sculptor working on site-specific work. She was the inventor of the 'wearable', the object which bridges the gap between jewellery and art
Studied: Falmouth School of Art, Cornwall, 1968–9; Central School of Art and Design, 1969–72
Collections: Crafts Council, London; Stedelijk Museum, Amsterdam; Victoria & Albert Museum, London

Martin Hopton
Own practice as a designer-jeweller and cabinet-maker since 1990, working on commissions for jewellery, watches and clocks
Studied: Central School of Art and Design, 1987–90
Part-time tutor on the jewellery course at Central Saint Martins from 1991 onwards
Collections: The Worshipful Company of Goldsmiths, London

Chris Howes
Own practice as a jeweller and silversmith, working on commissions for jewellery, watches and larger pieces. Collaborates with, and makes for, other designers
Studied: Birmingham College of Art, 1972–5
Part-time technician on the jewellery course at Central School of Art and Design, 1975–90. Senior technician at Central Saint Martins from 1990 onwards

Nuala Jamison
Own practice as a jeweller, working on a wide range of materials including silver, acrylic and textiles. Commissions include buttons and jewellery for fashion designer Jean Muir
Studied: Central School of Art and Design, 1969–72
Collections: Crafts Council, London

Giles Last
Own practice as a designer-jeweller and enameller. Designs both small- and large-scale pieces, also enamels for other designers
Studied: Central School of Art and Design, 1985–8; Barcelona, 1990–3
Full-time technician on the jewellery course at Central Saint Martins from 1994 onwards

John Leech
Retired senior technician at Central Saint Martins on the jewellery course
Studied: Central School of Art and Design, 1966–9
Technician, 1970–86

Sally Anne Lowe
Recently started own practice as a jeweller-designer, mainly working to commission for several retail outlets. Works part-time in Electrum Gallery
Studied: Central Saint Martins, 1989–93. Royal College of Art, 1993–5

Russell Lownsborough
Own jewellery practice since 1992, specialising in body-piercing jewellery. Designs for retail outlets include the Body Adornment Shop, working mainly in gold and silver. Worked as a craftsman for Jess James, 1991–2
Studied: Central Saint Martins, 1988–91

Peter Lyon
Long-established practice as a sculptor and jeweller. Sculpture work includes sculpture for Park Town Gardens, Oxford and for Cambridge University Engineering Department
Studied: Balliol College, Oxford; Edinburgh College of Art
Part-time tutor at Central School of Art and Design, 1966–9
Senior lecturer on the jewellery course at Central School of Art and Design, 1969–86

Jane McAdam Freud
Sculptor and medal engraver, including engraving for the Royal Mint
Studied: Wimbledon School of Art, 1976–7; Central School of Art and Design, 1978–81; Royal College of Art, 1993–5
Visiting tutor at the Royal College of Art from 1992 onwards
Collections: Berlin State Museum, Germany; British Museum, London; Rijksmuseum, Leiden, The Netherlands; The Worshipful Company of Goldsmiths, London

Tom McEwan
Precious jeweller, clients have included Kate Moss and Bruce Oldfield
Studied: Central School of Art and Design, 1979–82; Royal College of Art, 1983–6
Collections: World Gold Council Collection, The Worshipful Company of Goldsmiths, London

Julia Manheim
Sculptor and performance artist
Studied: Hornsey College of Art, London, 1967–8; Central School of Art and Design, 1969–72
Collections: Crafts Council, London; Stedelijk Museum, Amsterdam

Mick Milligan
Silversmith and jeweller, now only makes precious work to commission. Worked with Zandra Rhodes making fashion jewellery
Studied: Central School of Arts and Crafts, 1965; Royal College of Art, 1966–9
Part-time tutor on the jewellery course at Central School of Art and Design, 1978–9
Collections: The Worshipful Company of Goldsmiths, London

Neville Morgan
Industrial designer; previously worked with Robert Welch, silversmiths and the Rootes Group
Studied: Sculpture at Stoke School of Art, 1946–51; Royal College of Art, 1953–6
Worked on the jewellery course at Central School of Art and Design from 1967–96

Elizabeth Olver
Designer-jeweller, works mainly in precious materials
Studied: Central School of Art and Design, 1983–6; Royal
College of Art, 1994–6
Technician and subsequently tutor on the jewellery course at
Central Saint Martins, 1990–4 and 1996 onwards

Anna Opher
Designer-jeweller; works in silver, gold and gemstones
Studied: Central Saint Martins, 1991–4

Reema Pachachi
Designer-jeweller working in precious materials
Studied: Central School of Art and Design, 1973–6; Royal
College of Art, 1977–9
Part-time tutor on the jewellery course at Central Saint
Martins from 1995 onwards
Collections: Crafts Council, London

Gilian Packard
Designer-jeweller and lecturer. First Lady Freeman of the
Worshipful Company of Goldsmiths, 1971
Studied: Kingston College of Art, Surrey, 1955–7; Royal
College of Art, 1959–62
Tutor on the jewellery course at Central School of Art and
Design, 1965–78
Collections: The Worshipful Company of Goldsmiths,
London

Peter Page
Designer-jeweller and goldsmith, uses only precious
materials and works to commission. Freeman of the
Worshipful Company of Goldsmiths, 1980
Studied: Birmingham College of Art
Part-time tutor on the jewellery course at Central School of
Art and Design from 1972 onwards
Collections: The Worshipful Company of Goldsmiths,
London

Emma Paolozzi
Designer-jeweller, designs and makes precious jewellery for
Nicole Farhi and Paul Smith and works to commission
Studied: Central Saint Martins, 1988–91

Sara Pothecary
Goldsmith and jeweller, mainly works to commission
Studied: Central School of Art and Design, 1972–5; Royal
College of Art, 1975–8

Fiona Rae
Designer-jeweller and enameller
Studied: Central School of Art and Design, 1985–8
Part-time enamelling tutor at Central Saint Martins from
1991 onwards

Wendy Ramshaw OBE
Jeweller and sculptor, has worked in a variety of materials.
She is most famous for her ring sets. Freeman of The
Worshipful Company of Goldsmiths, 1973 and Liveryman,
1986
Studied: Newcastle upon Tyne College of Art and Industrial
Design, 1956–60; Reading University, 1960–1; Central
School of Art and Design, 1969
Collections: Crafts Council, London; Philadelphia Museum of
Art, USA; Schmuckmuseum, Pforzheim, Germany;
Museum of Industry, Oslo; The Museum of Modern Art,
Kyoto; Victoria & Albert Museum, London; The Worshipful
Company of Goldsmiths, London

Fred Rich
Goldsmith and enameller; works mainly to commission and
collaborates closely with Garrards, London. Freeman of The
Worshipful Company of Goldsmiths, 1994. Awards include
the Diamond International Award, 1988
Studied: Central School of Art and Design, 1978–81
Visiting Tutor on the jewellery course at Central Saint
Martins in 1980s and 1990s
Collections: The Worshipful Company of Goldsmiths,
London

Harriet Russell
Designer-jeweller and pattern-maker. Worked for Jess James
Studied: Central School of Art and Design, 1986–9

Tom Scott
Fine jeweller who has made work for firms such as Andrew Grima, Switzerland and Wartski, London. Freeman of The Worshipful Company of Goldsmiths, 1997
Studied: Hornsey College of Art, London, 1964–8
Part-time tutor on the jewellery course at Central School of Art and Design from 1974–86
Collections: The Worshipful Company of Goldsmiths, London

Jane Short
Enameller, silversmith and jeweller; works mainly to commission. Freeman of The Worshipful Company of Goldsmiths, 1984
Studied: Central School of Art and Design, 1972–5; Royal College of Art, 1975–8
Part-time tutor at Central School of Art and Design, 1979–95
Collections: Crafts Council, London; Victoria & Albert Museum, London; The Worshipful Company of Goldsmiths, London

Jos Skeates and **Ruaridh McIntyre**
Designer-jeweller partnership set up in 1996, generally using non-precious materials. Jos Skeates served a goldsmithing apprenticeship, 1986–91 and was made Freeman of The Worshipful Company of Goldsmiths, 1992
Studied: Both students at Central Saint Martins, 1993–6

Scilla Speet
Designer-jeweller and Course Director for the jewellery course at Central Saint Martins. Current interest in developing new silver alloys
Studied: Birmingham College of Art, 1967–70; Royal College of Art, 1970–3

Eric Spiller
Jeweller, interested in working with new technology and new materials. Head of Design at Robert Gordon University, Aberdeen
Studied: Central School of Art and Design, 1966–9; Royal College of Art, 1969–72
Collections: Crafts Council, London; Danner-Stiftung Collection, Munich

Ron Stevens
Designer-jeweller and silversmith
Studied: Gravesend School of Art, Kent, 1951–3; Royal College of Art 1954–7
Part-time tutor at Central School of Art and Design in the early 1960s
Full-time tutor on the jewellery course at Central School of Art and Design, 1966–97

Gerry Summers
Designer-jeweller; working in precious materials mainly to commission. Previous work includes a suite of jewellery for Diana Ross in 1984 and work made for Leo de Vroomen and David Thomas
Studied: Central School of Art and Design, 1977–80
Collections: The Worshipful Company of Goldsmiths, London

David Thomas
Goldsmith and designer-jeweller working in precious materials. Freeman of the Worshipful Company of Goldsmiths, 1966, and Liveryman, 1982. Past chairman of the Goldsmiths Crafts Council
Studied: Twickenham School of Art, Middlesex, 1952–6; Royal College of Art, 1958–61
Part-time tutor at Central School of Art and Design, 1963–5 and 1965–72
Collections: The Royal Museum of Scotland, Edinburgh; The Worshipful Company of Goldsmiths, London

Gunilla Treen
Jeweller working in a variety of materials including steel, titanium, aluminium, silver and plastic. Freewoman of The Worshipful Company of Goldsmiths, 1974. Set up the jewellery course at Morley College, London, 1971
Studied: Central School of Art and Design 1968–71
Collections: Crafts Council, London; Melbourne Museum, Victoria, Australia; Stedelijk Museum, Amsterdam, The Worshipful Company of Goldsmiths, London

Margaret Turner
Designer-jeweller with her own shops in London and Salisbury. Works in precious materials
Studied: Central School of Art and Design, 1974–7

John Volney
Designer-jeweller who also works as a craftsman for jewellers such as Liz Tyler. Works in silver and gold with gemstones
Studied: Central Saint Martins, 1991–4

Ginnie de Vroomen
Designer for De Vroomen Design set up in 1976 with her husband the goldsmith Leo de Vroomen. Creators of fine jewellery in precious materials, commercially and to commission. Freeman of The Worshipful Company of Goldsmiths, 1992
Studied: Central School of Art and Design, 1968–71
Collections: Victoria & Albert Museum, London; The Worshipful Company of Goldsmiths, London

Gary Wright and **Sheila Teague**
Jewellery designers and makers. Previous specialisation in silver, but now include 18-carat gold. Closely allied to fashion industry
Studied:
Gary Wright: Central School of Art and Design, 1972–5
Sheila Teague: Central School of Art and Design, 1972–4

Jewellers Interviewed

Jane Adam, interviewed by Janice West, Cockpit Workshop, London, 22 June 1997

Martin Baker, interviewed by Ron Stevens, Central Saint Martins College of Art and Design, London, 17 October 1996

Caroline Broadhead, interviewed by Ron Stevens, Middlesex University, 5 November 1996

Barbara Christie, interviewed by Ron Stevens, Central Saint Martins College of Art and Design, 29 October 1996

Ros Conway, interviewed by Ron Stevens, Middlesex University, 7 November 1996

Roger Doyle, interviewed by Ron Stevens, at his London workshop, 25 February 1997

Gerda Flöckinger, interviewed by Janice West, at her London workshop, 16 September 1997

Georgina Follett, interviewed by Ron Stevens, Central Saint Martins College of Art and Design, 21 January 1997

Simon Fraser, interviewed by Janice West, Central Saint Martins College of Art and Design, 22 October 1997

Graham Fuller, interviewed by Ron Stevens, Central Saint Martins College of Art and Design, 24 October 1996

Patrick Furse, interviewed by Ron Stevens, at his London studio, 3 December 1996

Dinny Hall, interviewed by Ron Stevens, at her Chelsea shop, 31 October 1996

Oonagh Hefford, interviewed by Ron Stevens, Central Saint Martins College of Art and Design, 4 December 1996

Susanna Heron, interviewed by Janice West, at her London studio, 19 September 1997

Martin Hopton, interviewed by Ron Stevens, Central Saint Martins College of Art and Design, 10 October 1996

Chris Howes, interviewed by Ron Stevens, Central Saint Martins College of Art and Design, 1 October 1996

Nuala Jamison, interviewed by Ron Stevens, at her London workshop, 9 December 1996

Giles Last, interviewed by Ron Stevens, Central Saint Martins College of Art and Design, 21 October 1996

John Leech, interviewed by Ron Stevens, Central Saint Martins College of Art and Design, 5 December 1996

Sally Anne Lowe, interviewed by Ron Stevens, at her Clerkenwell workshop, 9 December 1996

Russell Lownsborough, interviewed by Ron Stevens, at his Clerkenwell workshop, 18 November 1996

Peter Lyon, interviewed by Ron Stevens, Central Saint Martins College of Art and Design, 12 November 1996

Jane McAdam Freud, interviewed by Ron Stevens, at her South London Studio, 16 October 1996

Tom McEwan, interviewed by Ron Stevens, at his London workshop, 10 October 1996

Julia Manheim, interviewed by Ron Stevens, Kingsgate Workshops, London, 14 November 1996

Mick Milligan, interviewed by Ron Stevens, at his London workshop, 26 November 1996

Neville Morgan, interviewed by Ron Stevens, Central Saint Martins College of Art and Design, 2 December 1996

Elizabeth Olver, interviewed by Ron Stevens, Central Saint Martins College of Art and Design, 6 November 1996

Anna Opher, interviewed by Ron Stevens, at her Clerkenwell workshop, 5 December 1996

Reema Pachachi, interviewed by Ron Stevens, Central Saint Martins College of Art and Design, 7 October 1996

Gilian Packard, interviewed by Ron Stevens, Central Saint Martins College of Art and Design, 18 March 1997

Peter Page, interviewed by Ron Stevens, Central Saint Martins College of Art and Design, 2 October 1996

Emma Paolozzi, interviewed by Ron Stevens, Central Saint Martins College of Art and Design, 10 July 1997

Sara Pothecary, interviewed by Ron Stevens, Central Saint Martins College of Art and Design, 13 March 1997

Fiona Rae, interviewed by Ron Stevens, Central Saint Martins College of Art and Design, 14 October 1996

Wendy Ramshaw, interviewed by Ron Stevens, at her London studio, 5 March 1997

Fred Rich, interviewed by Ron Stevens, at his Surrey studio, 23 October 1996

Harriet Russell, interviewed by Ron Stevens, at her London workshop, 28 November 1996

Tom Scott, interviewed by Ron Stevens, at his London workshop, 27 November 1996

Jane Short, interviewed by Ron Stevens, at her Brighton workshop, 9 October 1996

Jos Skeates and Ruaridh McIntyre, interviewed by Ron Stevens, at their London workshop, 20 January 1997

Scilla Speet, interviewed by Ron Stevens, Central Saint Martins College of Art and Design, 24 October 1996 and interviewed by Janice West, Central Saint Martins College of Art and Design, 8 October 1997

Eric Spiller, interviewed by Janice West, Central Saint Martins College of Art and Design, 29 October 1997

Ron Stevens, interviewed by Janice West, Central Saint Martins College of Art and Design, 3 February 1997

Gerry Summers, interviewed by Ron Stevens, at his London workshop, 24 November 1996

David Thomas, interviewed by Ron Stevens, at his London workshop, 19 February 1997

Gunilla Treen, interviewed by Ron Stevens, at her Oxfordshire studio, 12 March 1997

Margaret Turner, interviewed by Ron Stevens, Central Saint Martins College of Art and Design, 13 March 1997

John Volney, interviewed by Ron Stevens, at his Clerkenwell workshop, 5 December 1996

Ginnie de Vroomen, interviewed by Janice West, at her Middlesex studio, 14 September 1997

Margarita Wood, interviewed by Janice West, at her London home, 12 September 1996

Gary Wright and Sheila Teague, interviewed by Ron Stevens, at their Clerkenwell workshop, 12 November 1996

Bibliography

Books

Anderson, Walter Truett, ed., *The Fontana Postmodernism Reader*, Fontana, 1996

Barthes, Roland, *Camera Lucida*, Fontana, 1982

Barthes, Roland, *The Fashion System*, University of California Press, 1990

Broadhead, Caroline, *New Tradition: The Evolution of Jewellery 1965–1985*, British Crafts Centre, 1985

Cartlidge, Barbara, *Twentieth Century Jewelry*, Abrams, 1985

Coleridge, Nicholas, *The Fashion Conspiracy*, Mandarin, 1989

Colette, *The Collected Short Stories of Colette*, translated by Matthew Ward, Penguin, 1985

Craik, Jennifer, *The Face of Fashion: Cultural Studies in Fashion*, Routledge, 1994

Dormer, Peter and Ralph Turner, *The New Jewelry, Trends and Traditions*, Thames and Hudson, 1985

Douglas, Mary, *Natural Symbols: Explorations in Cosmology*, Penguin, 1973

English, Helen Drutt and Peter Dormer, *Jewelry of Our Time: Art, Ornament and Obsession*, Thames and Hudson, 1995

Finkelstein, Joanne, *After a Fashion*, Melbourne University Press, 1996

Foster, Hal, ed., *Postmodern Culture*, Pluto Press, 1985

Frayling, Christopher, *The Royal College of Art: 150 Years of Art and Design*, Barrie and Jenkins, 1987

Heron, Susanna and David Ward, *The Jewellery Project*, Crafts Council, 1983

Hickey, Gloria, 'Craft within a consumer society' in *The Culture of Craft*, Manchester University Press, 1997

Hinks, Peter, *Twentieth-Century British Jewellery 1900–1980*, Faber and Faber, 1983

Houston, John, *Caroline Broadhead: Jewellery in Studio*, Bellew Publishing, 1990

Houston, John, ed., *Craft Classics since the 1940s*, Crafts Council, 1988

Hughes, Graham, *Modern Jewellery: an International Survey 1890–1963*, Studio Vista, 1963

Hughes, Graham, *The Art of Jewellery*, Studio Vista, 1972

Jewellery Redefined, exh. cat., British Craft Centre, 1982

Johnstone, William, *Points in Time, An Autobiography*, Barrie and Jenkins, 1980

Jones, Mark, *Contemporary British Medals*, British Museum Publications, 1986

London County Council, *Central School of Arts and Crafts Prospectus, 1963–64* and *1965–66*

London County Council, *Central School of Art and Design Prospectus 1966–67*

MacAdam Freud, Jane, *Sculpture: On the Edge*, Yorkshire Museum, 1996

Mack, John, *Ethnic Jewellery*, British Museum Press, 1988

Mulvagh, Jane, *Costume Jewelry in Vogue*, Thames and Hudson, 1988

Phillips, Clare, *Jewelry from Antiquity to the Present*, Thames and Hudson, 1996

Poston, David, *What is Jewellery?*, exh. cat., Crafts Council, 1995

Rhodes, Zandra and Anne Knight, *The Art of Zandra Rhodes*, Jonathan Cape, 1984

Rudofsky, Bernard, *The Unfashionable Human Body*, Hart Davis, 1972

Shining Through, exh. cat., Crafts Council, 1995

Turner, Ralph, *Jewelry in Europe and America: New Times, New Thinking*, Thames and Hudson, 1996

Untracht, Oppi, *Jewellery Concepts and Technology*, Robert Hale, 1982

Ward, David, *The Jewellery Project*, Crafts Council, 1983

Articles

Beasley, David, in *Goldsmiths' Review 1995–96*, Worshipful Company of Goldsmiths, 1996

Bennett, Alistair, 'The new primitives', *Variant*, no.16, Winter/Spring 1994

Brown, Mary Leavitt, 'Medal making at Central Saint Martins', *The Medal*, no.25, Autumn 1994

Evans, Caroline, 'Street style, subculture and subversion', *Costume*, no.31, 1997

Evans, James B., 'Silver and Electrum', *Metalsmith*, vol.17, no.2, Spring 1997

Fisher, Alexander, 'The art of enamelling upon metal', *The Studio*, 1906

Hill, Rosemary, 'Coating of many colours', *Crafts*, no.68, May/June 1984

Norton, Deborah, 'Caroline Broadhead: jewellery and beyond', *Metalsmith*, vol.14, no.1, Winter 1991

Poston, David, 'The medium is not the message', *Crafts*, no.68, May/June 1984

Rapley, Jane, 'Brian Wood's Obituary', *The Independent*, 14 September 1991

Slivka, Rose, 'New departures in jewellery', *Crafts*, no.64, September/October 1983

Periodicals

Aurum: the international gold magazine, published by the World Gold Council

Crafts: the decorative and applied arts magazine, published by the Crafts Council of England and Wales

Goldsmiths' Review: published by the Worshipful Company of Goldsmiths

The Medal: published by the British Art Medal Trust in association with FIDEM (Fédération Internationale de la Medaille)

Metalsmith: a publication of SNAG (Society of North-American Goldsmiths), an organisation for jewellers, designers and metalsmiths

Acknowledgements

Firstly, my thanks must go to Ron Stevens for his tireless interviewing and kindness.

I would also like to thank Sylvia Backemeyer and the Learning Resources staff at Central Saint Martins, David Beasley and his staff at the Worshipful Company of Goldsmiths' Library and the Information staff at the Crafts Council.

Friends and colleagues whose help has been invaluable are: Caroline Evans, Richard Mason, Caroline Dakers, Chris Washington-Sare, Karen Fletcher, Karen Wagstaff, Claire Barratt and Scilla Speet.

I must also extend my gratitude to Anjali Raval and her colleagues at Lund Humphries Publishers.

Lastly, my heartfelt thanks to all the people who have participated in this project; their knowledge, generosity and their enthusiasm have made it a pleasure.

This book is dedicated to my sister.

Janice West
Visiting tutor at Central Saint Martins College of Art and Design and Goldsmiths College, University of London.

Photographic Credits

The author and the publisher have made every effort to trace the copyright holders or owners of works and photographs. If any institutions or individuals have been incorrectly credited, or if there are any omissions, we would be glad to be notifed so that the necessary corrections can be made in any reprint.

Jane Adam 33
Martin Baker 37 (bottom, right)
Ed Barber 69 (right)
James Barlow 96 (bottom)
Caroline Broadhead 65
Douglas Cape 75
Barbara Christie 22-3, 34 (bottom)
Ros Conway 56 (top, right and left)
Bob Cramp 64 (right)
Joel Degen 33, 34 (bottom)
Gerda Flöckinger 12-13, 14, 15, 87, 88
Georgina Follett 25 (bottom, left and right)
Simon Fraser 32, 73, 75
Patrick Furse 43, 44, 45
John Gay 20 (both), 21 (both)
Hugo Glendenning 65
Dinny Hall 2, 93, 96 (both)
Mike Hallsam 64 (left)
Susanna Heron 58-9, 67 (both), 68 (top)
Elizabeth Holder 37 (top, right), 56 (top, right)
Martin Hopton 37 (top, right)
Chris Howes 37 (top, left)
Nuala Jamison 92 (top and bottom)
Giles Last 56 (bottom, right and left)
Sally Anne Lowe 103 (bottom, right and left)
Russell Lownsborough 110 (both)
Peter Lyon 60
Jane McAdam Freud 80 (both), 81
Julia Manheim 69 (both), 72
Jean Muir Ltd 92 (bottom)
Graham Murrell 36 (bottom, right and left)

Elizabeth Olver 99 (bottom, right)
Anna Opher 103 (top)
Reema Pachachi 82-3, 89
Peter Page 40 (all), 85
Emma Paolozzi 76, 107 (both)
Keith Pattison 69 (left)
Fiona Rae 57 (both)
Wendy Ramshaw 64 (right)
Fred Rich 53
Llewellyn Robin 40 (all), 85
Constantino Ruspoli 2, 96 (top)
Skeates and McIntyre 106 (all)
Rose Smith 82-3, 89
Scilla Speet 36 (bottom, right and left)
Eric Spiller 41 (both)
Frank Thurston 76, 107 (both)
Gunilla Treen 68 (bottom)
Margaret Turner 28 (left)
John Volney 28 (right)
De Vroomen Design Ltd 29 (top, left and right), 52
David Ward 58-9, 67 (both), 68 (top)
Simon Wheeler 102 (both)
Margarita Woods 20 (both), 21 (both)
The Worshipful Company of Drapers 37 (bottom, left)
The Worshipful Company of Goldsmiths 17, 18, 25 (top, left and right), 29 (bottom), 34 (top), 36 (top), 48, 49 (both), 61 (both), 77 (all), 98, 99 (top and bottom left)
Wright and Teague 102 (both)

Index